M000012335

FOOD THAT ROCKS

FOOD THAT ROCKS

Favorite Recipes from the Hottest Kitchens in Music

MARGIE LAPANJA & CINDY COVERDALE

CONARI
PRESS

First published in 2004 by Conari Press,
an imprint of Red Wheel/Weiser, LLC
York Beach, ME
With offices at:
368 Congress Street
Boston, MA 02210
www.redwheelweiser.com

Copyright © 2004 Margie Beiser Lapanja and Cindy Coverdale

All rights reserved. No part of this publication may be reproduced or transmitted in any form or by any means, electronic or mechanical, including photocopying, recording, or by any information storage and retrieval system, without permission in writing from Red Wheel/Weiser, LLC. Reviewers may quote brief passages.

Library of Congress Cataloging-in-Publication Data

Lapanja, Margie.
  Food that rocks / Margie Lapanja and Cindy Coverdale.
    p. cm.
  ISBN 1-57324-908-4 (alk. paper)
  1. Cookery. 2. Rock musicians. I. Coverdale, Cindy. II. Title.
  TX714.L355 2004
  641.5--dc22
                      2003016936

Cover design: Garrett Brown
Author photograph: Zweigle/Ratiner Studios
Interior design and typesetting: Garrett Brown

Printed in the United States of America
Malloy

11 10 09 08 07 06 05 04
8 7 6 5 4 3 2 1

The paper used in this publication meets the minimum requirements of the American National Standard for Information Sciences-Permanence of Paper for Printed Library Materials Z39.48-1992 (R1997).

To Michael Joseph Beiser,
My star who rocks.

—Sist☆r Margaret Mary

To my boys, David and Jasper . . .
You make my heart sing!

—Cindy

If music be the food of love,

play on!

—Shakespeare, *Twelfth Night*

Contents

Chapter 2 Special Guest 45

Sizzlin' Sides and a Pasta Performance

Shania's Potato Roast—Shania Twain

Potatoes Gratin with Bacon, Arugula, and Caramelized Onions—Doug Aldrich

Green Tips Asparagus Vinaigrette with Poached Egg Mousseline
—Chef Yves Gigot of La Ferme

Spanakopita—Timothy Drury

Donatella's Special Tuna Pasta—Leo Sayer

Joe's Italian Meat Sauce for Pasta—Joe Lynn Turner

Stevie's Meatballs—Steve Hamilton

Pasta Alle Bossi with Pizza Bread—Doug Bossi

Spicy Chicken Pasta—Eric Singer

Seared Tuna with Pasta—Peter Rivera

Linguine and Clams Castellamare—Frankie Banali

Shrimp with Pasta in Sour Cream and Tomato Sauce—Larry Hoppen

Shrimp Scampi Pasta—Joe Satriani

Pappardelle Genovese—Andy Hamilton

The "Sizzling Penne & Double Truffle" Blues Gratin—Adrian Vandenberg

Electrifying Entrées

Caramelised Halibut with Parmesan and Herb Gnocchi, Mousserons, and Sweetcorn Velouté—*The Tea Room at The Clarence*

Seared Hawaiian Ahi with Japanese Salsa—*Croce's Restaurant*

Grilled Sea Bass—*Doug "Cosmo" Clifford*

Ginger–Lime–Cilantro Marinade with Halibut—*Chef Colby Leonard for Mike Love*

Vinster Codzoni—*Vinnie Pantaleoni*

Zen Master DJ Mix—*Max Volume*

Whole Fresh Salmon à la Chinese Style—*Tony Hadley*

Ty Peanut Sauce with Rice and Veggies—*Tyler Haugum*

Not My Curry Recipe—*John Wesley Harding*

Chicken Saltimbocca—*Patti Russo*

Chicken Escalope with Cajun Mustard Sauce—*Paul Young*

Uncle Spikey's "Honeylamb" Chili—*Spike Edney*

Lamb Rogan Josh—*John Lodge*

John X's Big, Fat, Greek Leg of Lamb with Occasional Potato—*John X*

Veal with Lime Sauce—*Reb Beach*

Chile Maple Glazed Pork Tenderloin with Braised Red Cabbage and Sweet Potato Purée—*Joey Altman*

Derek's Burritos—*Derek Hilland*

Southern Sloppy Buffalo Burgers—*Rickey Medlocke*

Show Time!

Introduction

Welcome to the show!

It is our great pleasure to present *Food That Rocks*—a delicious tribute to food and music and to everyone who loves to *cook!* You are about to experience a culinary concert of favorite food, makes-you-want-to-get-up-and-dance food, and food that feeds your soul.

And you are in good company: *Food That Rocks* is a benefit concert cooked up to assist Freedom from Hunger, a charitable organization that helps women and their families in developing countries break free from poverty. Every contributor gave freely of his or her time, sharing culinary secrets and signature recipes. With their help, we have created a big, bountiful feast for all to enjoy, and for this we are so very grateful.

At this show, everyone gets a front row seat *and* a backstage pass for an intimate "meet and greet" with all the players who contributed. Our line-up includes a sensational smorgasbord of superstars to session players, divas to disc jockeys, and a full house of musical epicures who bring their rich gifts and talents to the table, dedicated to adding more zest and flavor to life. We also give a spotlight to musician-owned restaurants, cookbooks penned by musicians, writers who rock, and chefs who jam!

Because we want you to be thoroughly entertained, we've preserved the eclectic nature and charming flair of each recipe by printing *it* in the voice in which *it* came to us from our contributors, complete with personal annotations, frisky remarks, and international idioms. Along with enlightening and practical "Rehearsal Notes" following an occasional dish to ensure that your kitchen concert is most enjoyable, you will also find handy metric-to-English unit conversions for those rollicking recipes given to us by our British and European friends.

The opening act is sure to delight, with signature salads, soups, and amped-up appetizers like Patti LaBelle's Potato Salad, David Coverdale's favorite Soulful Shrimp Soup, and a rockin' version of Marco Mendoza's Mama's Ceviche. While former Pumpkin front man Billy Corgan sets the stage with his smashing version of Russian Salad, special guests Shania Twain, Leo Sayer, and Joe Satriani, among others, turn up the heat with sizzling side dishes and perfect-performance pasta to tantalize the taste buds just in time for the headliner.

You definitely won't be saying, "I can't get no satisfaction," with the electrifying entrées served up next at this party. Satiate your senses with a Garlic Rubbed Rock & Roll Rib Steak, Seared Hawaiian Ahi with Japanese Salsa from Croce's Restaurant, or an off-the-charts version of Ted Nugent's Bubble Bean Piranha à la Colorado Moose before indulging in the finale of desserts worthy of a standing ovation. Brian May's Mum's Blackberry Purée and Sarah McLachlan's Currant Cake will surely entertain your tummy, in case the Cherry Garcia Phish Food in One Sweet Whirled Rockin' Hot Fudge Sundae doesn't.

Finally, for a delicious mix of style and tastes, be sure to treat yourself to the exciting jam session that follows: Jennifer Lopez leads the jam and cooks with a favorite home-spun meal of Empañadas Fritas, Crema De Frijoles Negros, and Arroz Con Pollo from her fêted restaurant, Madre's. Joe Perry of Aerosmith will Rock Your World with his Steak & Eggs, Bob Weir adds some Snake Oil Stir Fry to his Peanut Satay Sauce, and Steve Vai tops it all with Steve's Sticky Banana.

Food That Rocks is guaranteed to chase away the blues and satisfy your senses the good old-fashioned way—great music, outstanding food, and excellent company. So ladies and gentlemen, join us now for a fun-filled musical feast and grand celebration of rock 'n' roll cuisine. Grab an apron and your favorite tunes, turn up the volume, fire up the stove, and let the show begin!

Chapter 1

Opening Act

Signature Salads, Soups, and Amped-up Appetizers

Potato Salad—Patti LaBelle

Asian Chicken Salad—Eric Martin

Spicy Coleslaw—Doug Aldrich

Pork Tenderloin Salad—Doug Aldrich

Tour Bus Tuna—Leslie West

Russian Salad—Billy Corgan

Brussels Sprouts Salad—Gordon Drysdale

Sweet Potato–Plantain Soup with Coconut and Rum Cream—Joey Altman

Yucatan Pork Chile—Joey Altman

Soulful Shrimp Soup—David Coverdale

Pea Soup—Nate Mendel

Basic Bread—Bob Kastelic

Potato Leek Soup—Tommy Aldridge

Curried Pumpkin Soup—Gregg Bissonette

Spicy Chicken Wingers—Reb Beach

Baked Stuffed Avocados—Chuck Bürgi

Mama's Ceviche—Marco Mendoza

Patti LaBelle

From the time I was a little girl, I knew there were two things in this world I was born to do: sing and cook.

—Patti LaBelle

When "Lady Marmalade" cooks, she *cooks!* This "soulful diva extraordinaire" heats up the kitchen, stage, and the world with her warmth, enthusiasm, and unbridled optimism. In addition to her newest CD, *When a Woman Loves*, and the thirty-plus albums she's recorded in various incarnations (in the '60s as leader of Patti LaBelle & the Bluebelles; in the '70s with Labelle; and since 1977, as a soloist), Patti has established herself as a bestselling author, inspirational spokesperson, and artist-development manager.

Her books—*LaBelle Cuisine, Patti LaBelle's Lite Cuisine, Don't Block the Blessings,* and *Patti's Pearls*—highlight her passion for cooking and living wisely and well. Pattonium Management, based out of her hometown of Philadelphia, is Patti's way of reciprocating her life's gifts: "I still have so much more to do, so many other things to try. I have a lot of blessings, a lot to be thankful for . . . but I'm always excited about what else there is for me to do. My desire is to help young and talented artists achieve the kind of success that I've been fortunate enough to experience throughout my career."

And to this she adds, "Now get your apron, Sugar, and let's do some cooking, Patti-style."

Backstage with Patti LaBelle . . .

If you were a food, what would you be?

An extra-jumbo hard-shell Maryland male crab with lots of spice on him!

What is your favorite food?

Pasta.

Do you have a favorite restaurant?

The Cheesecake Factory. My favorite items on the menu are the crabcakes, calamari, all the cheesecakes, and the sliders.

Have you written/recorded a song with a food theme or title?

"Lady Marmalade."

Do you have any special "backstage food" requests?

[That there is] an assortment of seafood.

Do you have a signature dish you like to cook or serve?

Potato Salad (recipe follows).

What song would you recommend playing while preparing this?

"I Believe I Can Fly."

Potato Salad

20 large Yukon Gold or "all-purpose" red potatoes, boiled and diced

One dozen large eggs, hard-boiled

2 medium Vidalia or Bermuda onions, finely chopped

1 large green bell pepper, diced into small pieces

3 stalks celery, diced into small pieces

½ cup sweet relish

1 cup Hellmann's mayonnaise (approximately)

4 to 6 tablespoons French's yellow mustard

1 tablespoon cayenne pepper

1 habañero pepper, finely chopped (optional)

Celery seed, to taste

Lawry's Seasoned Salt, to taste

Paprika, as garnish

Hard-boil the eggs (see Rehearsal Notes following). Boil potatoes (with or without skin) in a large pot of water until you can stick a fork into them and it goes in easily, approximately 20 to 25 minutes. When the potatoes are done, remove from water, remove the skins, and dice into bite-sized chunks.

Slice the eggs into large chunks (they will crumble when you are mixing the salad). Reserve a few slices to use as a garnish.

Place the potatoes and eggs in an extra-large bowl and gently fold in onions, green pepper, celery, and relish. Add the mayonnaise and mustard, mixing gently (the salad should be "wet" but not "runny"). Finally, add the cayenne pepper and habañero pepper, if using, and season with celery seed and Lawry's salt according to taste. Stir all of the ingredients together.

Garnish with large slices of hard-boiled egg and paprika. Refrigerate until ready to serve. Enjoy! Makes 15 to 20 servings.

Rehearsal Notes

♪ In her cookbook, *LaBelle Cuisine*, Patti demystifies the secret for perfect hard-boiled eggs:

> I know that most people actually boil their eggs to hard-cook them, but if you overdo it, you get that thin green line around the yolk that everyone just hates. Here's the foolproof professional way to hard-cook eggs that cuts down on the actual boiling time to avoid overcooking.
>
> Place the eggs in a saucepan just large enough to hold them in one layer. Fill with enough cold water to cover by 1 inch. Bring to a gentle boil over high heat. Cook for 30 seconds. Remove from the stove and cover tightly. Let stand for 15 minutes. Pour out most of the water and place the pan in the sink. Let cold water run over the eggs for about 3 minutes. Crack and peel the eggs while still warm.

♪ As all mayonnaise connoisseurs know, Hellmann's is "known as Best Foods west of the Mississippi."

Eric Martin

What more can be said about man who avows, "Life couldn't be better. I have a loving wife, a pool, a six-pack o' Guinness in the fridge, and a guitar on my lap"? That he *is* Mr. Big and that the "loving wife" is also the talented Eric Martin Band drummer, Denise Martin. And that the EMB has come full circle—launching its debut *Sucker for a Pretty Face* in 1983, then transforming into the wildly successful Mr. Big (with singer Eric Martin still holding the tune) throughout the late '80s into the new millennium, and now once again rocking as the Eric Martin Band.

We definitely know Japan loves him. In 1999 Mr. Big released *Get Over It* in Japan, played a rousing New Year's Eve show with Aerosmith at the Osaka Dome in Tokyo, and then watched *Get Over It* go multi-platinum there while yielding a number one hit, "Superfantastic," along the way. And we are excited to say Eric Martin and his "signature soulful voice" are now back in the U.S.A. celebrating *I'm Goin' Sane*, the revitalized band's new CD.

Backstage with Eric Martin . . .

If you were a food, what would you be?

I would be the all-knowing, all-seeing carrot!

What is your favorite food?

Italian and Japanese.

Favorite restaurant . . . Favorite item on the menu?

Sushi to Dai For in San Rafael, California . . . Bonito Tuna Sashimi and the Pork Tonkatsu.

Have you written or recorded a song with a food theme or title?

No, but I've hungered for love all my life.

Special "backstage food" requests . . .

I pretty much get the usual: Deli tray and beer. But in a perfect world: Thai food and sake with some green tea ice cream.

What song would you recommend to accompany your recipe?

"Stone in Love" by Journey . . . Motown or Stax/Volt [music labels].

My wife, Denise Martin, is a great cook. I love her recipe for Asian Chicken Salad.

Asian Chicken Salad

2 large chicken breasts, skinned and deboned

One 3-ounce package Asian rice noodles, crushed into small pieces

1 head lettuce, shredded

5 green onions, chopped

1 cucumber, sliced

2½ tablespoons slivered almonds

¾ tablespoon sesame seeds

Mandarin oranges (optional)

The Dressing

⅓ cup vegetable oil

3½ tablespoons vinegar

2¼ tablespoons sugar (or less, to taste)

2¼ tablespoons lemon juice

1 tablespoon peeled ginger root

¾ teaspoon salt

½ teaspoon pepper

In a large saucepan, simmer chicken breasts in water over medium-low heat for about 25 minutes or until tender. Remove chicken and let cool. Shred and set aside.

Break the Asian rice noodles into small pieces by crushing the package. Follow the directions on the noodle package to cook (except substitute water for oil).

Combine remaining salad ingredients—lettuce, green onions, cucumber, almonds, sesame seeds, and mandarin oranges, if using—with chicken and noodles.

Prepare dressing by whisking all ingredients together. Toss with salad immediately. Best if served cold. Makes 4 servings.

Doug Aldrich

Doug Aldrich is blessed with an extraordinary talent for guitar playing and an exceptional feel for technique and melody. For Doug, freeing the music his guitar has to offer is not simply a job or a hobby, but a way of life. His commitment is total. Onstage he moves gracefully—as if the guitar and he are one—proving beyond a doubt that *this is* where he belongs.

His first acknowledged successful band was Lion, followed by stints with Hurricane, House of Lords, and Burning Rain. His guitar wizardry, featured on *Killing the Dragon* by the heavy metal band Dio, also works its mojo on several attention-grabbing solo albums. In 2003 Doug took the stage as a member of Whitesnake, a band known for its outstanding rock guitarists.

Staying true to his influences, the great exponents of the electric guitar—Jimi Hendrix, Eric Clapton, Jeff Beck, Jimmy Page, and Edward Van Halen—Aldrich exudes an enduring confidence in his playing and performing that transcends more fashionable movements in music. He proudly notes, "Musically I still listen to the old music, because I don't want to lose my roots. I'm not one of those guys who is interested in following whatever is trendy. I'd rather stick to what I do best and do it to the best of my ability."

Backstage with Doug Aldrich . . .

If you were a food, what would you be?

Steak.

What is your favorite food?

Japanese sashimi.

Your favorite restaurant . . . Favorite item on the menu?

Matsuhisu in Los Angeles . . . Everything is great—the Tuna Tataki Salad!

Do you have any special "backstage food" requests?

Just healthy foods: fish or chicken and baked potato

Spicy Coleslaw

1 teaspoon cumin seeds

1 teaspoon coriander seeds

1 cup mayonnaise

½ to 1 habañero pepper, seeded, finely chopped

3 tablespoons canned green chiles, finely chopped

2 garlic cloves, finely chopped

2 to 3 tablespoons fresh lime juice

2 tablespoons pure maple syrup

1 tablespoon cilantro, finely chopped

1 tablespoon Worcestershire sauce

1 tablespoon Dijon mustard

1 tablespoon apple cider vinegar

Salt

5 cups green cabbage, shredded

3 cups purple cabbage, shredded

2 medium carrots, shredded

In a small dry skillet, toast cumin and coriander seeds over medium heat until fragrant (about 2 minutes). Let cool, then grind in a mortar or spice grinder.

In a blender or food processor, combine the remaining ingredients except for both cabbages and carrots. Season with salt. (This dressing can be refrigerated for up to one day.)

In a large bowl, combine both cabbages and carrots with dressing, toss well to coat, and refrigerate for 2 hours or more until chilled. Serves 6 to 8.

Pork Tenderloin Salad

1 pound pork tenderloin

Assorted mixed greens

1 bunch asparagus, blanched

1 red pepper, sliced

1 avocado, sliced

Marinade

½ cup soy sauce

¼ cup Oriental sesame oil

¼ cup sugar

¼ cup pineapple, diced

2 cloves garlic, minced

1 teaspoon red chile flakes

Combine soy sauce, sesame oil, sugar, pineapple, garlic, and red chili flakes in a bowl, pour over pork, and marinate overnight. (I like to use an airtight, resealable plastic bag.)

Honey Ginger Dressing

¼ cup peanut oil

3 tablespoons balsamic or red wine vinegar

2 teaspoons honey

1 teaspoon minced ginger

1 teaspoon Dijon mustard

Salt and pepper to taste

Whisk oil, vinegar, honey, ginger, mustard together in a bowl. Season with salt and pepper. (Dressing can be made up to one day ahead.)

Cooking and serving:

Heat grill and cook marinated tenderloin until cooked through, about 6 minutes per side. Transfer meat to plate and let rest for 5 minutes.

Arrange mixed greens and blanched asparagus on a platter. Cut pork across the grain and arrange over the greens. Scatter the red peppers and avocado around the meat and drizzle with the vinaigrette. Bon appetit! Makes 4 servings.

Leslie West

Prodigious blues-rock guitarist and singer Leslie West is perhaps best known for his involvement with the unforgettable '70s band Mountain, considered by many to be the only serious rival to the legendary progressive blues band Cream, which featured the one and only Eric Clapton on guitar. In fact, Leslie West and Cream bass player extraordinaire Jack Bruce actually worked together in the well remembered West, Bruce, and Laing, featuring Leslie's best friend Corky Laing on drums.

Leslie was first exposed to guitar playing when his grandmother took him to see a taping of *The Jackie Gleason Show*, where his uncle was a writer. After they arrived, that day's show was cancelled, and instead Leslie found himself in the studio audience for the first television broadcast of Elvis Presley! From that moment, he began playing the guitar every day and never stopped.

As well as being a guitar teacher and designer, Leslie continues to tour as a solo performer, flying the flag of progressive blues and thrilling audiences wherever he appears.

Backstage with Leslie West . . .

If you were a food, what would you be?

I would be any kind of food so people could just *"Eat Me!"*

What is your favorite food?

British bangers!

What is your favorite restaurant?

Since my brother Larry owns several restaurants and my cousin Mike owns thirty restaurants—an array of all kinds—in New York City, any one of them: Rigoletto's is Italian.

New York-New York Hotel in Las Vegas [where there] are thirteen restaurants, including the world-famous Stage Deli. No wonder I got so fat years ago!

Do you have any special "backstage food" requests?

I don't care what food is backstage really. It is not for me anyway; just [for] all the moochers.

Tour Bus Tuna

This is serious tuna salad. We used to have contests on the tour bus as to who made the best. Guess who always won? Not Charlie Tuna! This version was always a hit.

One 6-ounce can tuna, drained

¾ cup celery, chopped

½ cup almonds, chopped or sliced

¼ cup red onion, chopped

2 tablespoons Miracle Whip (approximately)

A little pickle juice, to taste

A little Dijon mustard, to taste

3 to 4 brioche rolls (brown bread or onion rolls will do in a pinch)

Combine all ingredients and serve on rolls.

Billy Corgan

The Smashing Pumpkins exploded onto the music scene in Chicago in 1988, with founding member Billy Corgan re-centering the musical map with his forceful vocals and raw song-writing talent. The Pumpkins became the longest-running and most successful of the '90s alt-rock bands, merging Gen-X metal with an alternative sound and tying it all up with an experimental, psychedelic twist. Best known for their 1993 classic *Siamese Dream* and multi-platinum *Mellon Collie* albums, they enthralled a whole new generation of listeners who were searching, testing.

By the new millennium, William Patrick Corgan Jr. had heard a different drummer. After disbanding the Smashing Pumpkins with a marathon retrospective finale at Chicago's Metro in December 2000, Corgan reemerged on the sunny side of the street with his new band Zwan (Japanese for "design"). Their first album, *Mary Star of the Sea*, its cover smiling with rainbows and a dove, debuted at #3. While Corgan still delivers powerful lyrics over full-amp rock, his new songs invoke the "Let It Be" spirit of the Love Generation and redeem the restlessness of Gen X.

Backstage with Billy Corgan . . .

If you were a food, what would you be?

Cumquat.

What is your favorite food?

French fries.

Do you have a favorite restaurant . . . Favorite item on the menu?

Carmine's in Chicago . . . the Flat-noodle Pasta.

Food for thought . . .

I love food! As my friend Matt says, "Good food is the one thing in life you can count on!"

What music would you recommend to accompany your recipe?

Howlin' Wolf—Sun Sessions.

Russian Salad

2 large potatoes, boiled, cooled, and chopped into small cubes

4 eggs, hard-boiled, cooled, and chopped into small cubes

3 scallions, chopped into small pieces

2 cucumbers, chopped into small cubes

4 sweet pickles, chopped into small cubes

One 8-ounce can sweet green peas

Salt to taste

Mayonnaise to taste

Prepare the potatoes and eggs. In a large bowl, "mix it all up"—the potatoes, eggs, scallions, cucumbers, and pickles. Then add the sweet green peas and mix again. Add salt and mayonnaise before serving. Makes 6 to 8 servings.

Gordon Drysdale and Joey Altman

There's a line from a song, "Keep your day job 'til your night job pays," but a bunch of chef-musicians from the San Francisco Bay Area who are heating up the town with their Back Burner Blues Band *and* who happen to operate some of the finest eateries around might not know which gig is what job anymore.

Two singing, guitar-toting master chefs, Joey Altman (see pages 151 and 188) and mandolin *artiste* Gordon Drysdale (page 232) are cookin' in more ways than one with drummer-chef Keith Luce of Merenda, lead guitarist-vocalist Scott Warner from Bistro Don Giovanni in Napa, Andre Chapital, San Francisco fireman and gumshoe-gourmet (and occasional bartender at the Acme Chop House) holding the tune, and "pizza man" ringer Mike Sweetland playing stand-up bass. So next time you're in the City by the Bay, treat yourself to their blues-based jazz-rock-bluegrass-funk—or their food.

Brussels Sprouts Salad

Chef Gordon Drysdale

Our most requested recipe ever: impossibly, it is the Warm Brussels Sprouts Salad, and it is universally beloved.

½ pound slab bacon, cut into ¼-inch squares

2 medium onions, peeled and sliced

2 tablespoons canola oil

6 slices country-style bread, crusts removed and cut in ½-inch squares

2 tablespoons extra-virgin olive oil

6 large eggs, prepared (see following)

2 to 3 pounds Brussels sprouts (should have about 40 sprouts)

3 tablespoons canola oil (for cooking salad)

Early in the day, prepare the mise en place:

Cut bacon and cook over low heat until almost crisp; drain off most of fat and set aside. Heat 2 tablespoons canola oil until just smoking and cook sliced onions over medium-high heat until golden brown. Drain and set aside.

Toss cubed bread with extra-virgin olive oil and toast in a 300°F oven until golden brown and crispy (approximately 20 to 25 minutes). Allow to cool to room temperature and set aside.

Cover the eggs with cold water in a large saucepan, bring to scald, and let sit in scalding water for 8 to 9 minutes. Run cold water over eggs to stop cooking—be sure yolk is firm but a little undercooked—peel and cut into ⅛ths. Reserve, covered, in the refrigerator.

Also, early in the day prepare your vinaigrette:

Vinaigrette

3 tablespoons red wine vinegar

½ cup canola oil

1 large clove garlic, minced

1 large shallot, minced

2 teaspoons fresh thyme leaves

Salt and pepper to taste

Soak the garlic, shallots, and thyme in the vinegar for 45 minutes, more or less, and slowly whisk in the oil. Season to taste with salt and pepper and reserve, covered, for service.

While all the other items are "working," clean the sprouts:

Remove the first few dark leaves and discard. Cut off the stem and separate the leaves one by one (this is not particularly fun). When you get to the light green center and can't pull off the leaves, either slice the heart very thin or reserve for other uses.

To cook the salad (finally!):

In a large sauté pan, heat remaining canola oil until almost smoking and add leaves. Toss until wilted (3 to 4 minutes), season with salt and pepper, then add reserved onions and bacon and toss until hot.

When hot, add vinaigrette, toss to distribute and taste for seasoning. When seasoned correctly, add croutons and chopped eggs, toss to incorporate, and serve! Makes 4 servings.

Sweet Potato—Plantain Soup with Coconut and Rum Cream

Chef Joey Altman

3 yellow onions, finely sliced

6 sweet potatoes, peeled and sliced ¼-inch thick

4 plantains (ripe, dark-yellowish red to brown), peeled, sliced ½-inch thick

Two 14-ounce cans coconut milk

2 tablespoons ginger, minced

3 quarts chicken stock

1 quart heavy cream

¼ pound butter

Salt and pepper to taste

½ cup lime juice (lemon will do fine)

In a 2-gallon (or larger) stockpot, sweat onions till they are lightly browned. Add sweet potatoes, plantains, coconut milk, ginger, chicken stock, and 1 quart of cream. Simmer until the potatoes are very soft. Purée, whisk in the butter, and season with salt and pepper. Add lime juice if needed.

Coconut and Rum Cream

1 cup heavy cream

½ cup rum

¼ teaspoon ground allspice

¼ teaspoon ground nutmeg

½ cup toasted hazelnuts

In a bowl, whip cream to a "soft peaks" consistency and fold in rum, allspice, and nutmeg.

Pour hot soup into bowls and garnish with a dollop of whipped cream and hazelnuts. Makes 6 to 8 servings.

Yucatan Pork Chile

Chef Joey Altman

1 pound pork shoulder, cut in ½-inch cubes, lightly seasoned with kosher salt and pepper to taste

2 tablespoons vegetable oil or lard

2 cups yellow onions, diced medium

2 cups fresh poblaño chile peppers, diced medium

½ cup garlic, minced

2 cups yucca, peeled, diced small

2 cups tomatillos, quartered

2 cups orange juice

2 bottles dark Mexican beer (Negro Modelo)

1 teaspoon cumin seed, toasted and ground

½ cup fresh cilantro

Garnishes: Mexican sour cream, tomato salsa, fried corn tortilla shards, chili powder, salt, a few sprigs of fresh cilantro

In a heavy-bottomed pot with a tight-fitting lid, sear the pork over medium-high heat in the oil or lard, browning the meat. Transfer the meat to a bowl with a slotted spoon or a pair of tongs.

Add the onion and chile peppers to the pot and cook, stirring frequently, until the onions are caramelized to a nice golden brown. Add the garlic and continue cooking for 2 more minutes. Add the yucca, tomatillos, orange juice, beer, and cumin. Bring to a boil. Turn the heat down to a simmer, add the meat back in, and cover. Stew, stirring and skimming off fat occasionally, for 2 hours. During the last 10 minutes of cooking stir in the cilantro. (The stew should be thick; add water if it gets too dry.)

Top with a dollop of fresh Mexican sour cream and a small spoonful of tomato salsa and garnish by sticking fried corn tortilla shards dusted with chili powder and salt into the center of the cream and salsa. Lay a few sprigs of fresh cilantro over them. Serves 4.

David Coverdale

David Coverdale's voice is his great gift: bluesy and soulful, he can command it to soar from a whisper to a scream in the space of a bar and overwhelm you with its raw, passionate emotion. And then, oh-so-masterfully, he hands your heart back to you with a wistful, more soothing note from a classic ballad. At once captivating and connecting, it is this hallmark of his music that his audiences adore. Coverdale *shines* on stage.

David set his professional career in motion in 1973 when he, then a British "unknown," auditioned successfully as lead singer for Deep Purple, one of the world's greatest bands at that time. After exceeding all personal and professional expectations, he left Deep Purple to form his own band, Whitesnake. Their first album was released in 1978. Propelled by David's powerful voice and song-writing talent, perfectly complemented with a hot 'n' heavy line-up of stellar musicians, Whitesnake rocked the charts. With hits like "Is This Love?" and "Here I Go Again," they filled stadium after stadium.

After enjoying over twenty years of international success with Whitesnake, David took a break to collaborate with Led Zeppelin's guitar legend Jimmy Page. The critically acclaimed *Coverdale/Page* album, a showcase of brilliant talent, hit platinum. He followed this with a solo album *Into the Light*, and in 2003, after hearing the call to return to the stage, regrouped Whitesnake for a vastly successful Silver Anniversary world-tour celebration.

Backstage with David Coverdale . . .

If you were a food, what would you be?

An artichoke, because it is a delicious journey and it takes patience to actually get to the *heart*, but once you do . . . *look out!*

What is your favorite food?

Vegaquarian (seafood-vegetarian).

Do you have a favorite restaurant . . . Favorite items on the menu?

La Ferme, in Genoa, Nevada. . . . The Asparagus with Poached Egg [enjoy the experience on page 51] and the Seafood Bouillabaisse.

McCoy's Restaurant in Cleveland, England. . . . The Sticky Toffee Pudding Cake is amazing! [This recipe is on page 186.]

And, *all* of Marco Pierre White's London restaurants! . . . Everything, that is, but the "Pigs Trotter"!

Do you have special "backstage food" requests?

Sushi, sake, Puligny and Chassagne Montrachet wine, French Cognac . . . oh yes, tea—green and black—lots of it!

Have you ever written or recorded a song with a food theme or title?

"Wine, Women and Song" and "Bloody Mary" (meal in a glass!).

What music would you recommend to accompany your recipe?

The music of good conversation, with a bit of baroque thrown in for good measure!

Anything else food or music related you would like to add?

If music be the food of love . . . Play on, Maestro!

Soulful Shrimp Soup

This culinary delight comes from Laura Velasco, who has cooked many a fine meal for us in our home. It is absolutely delicious and fresh tasting, and goes very nicely with Mama's Ceviche [on page 42].

1 pound large, uncooked shrimp, peeled and deveined

2 tomatoes, chopped

½ cucumber, peeled and chopped

½ avocado, chopped

4 tablespoons ketchup

3 tablespoons cilantro, finely chopped

2 tablespoons onion, chopped

Juice of ½ lime

Prepare shrimp and set aside. Combine tomatoes, cucumber, avocado, ketchup, cilantro, onion, and lime juice in a bowl and set aside.

Purée

1 tomato

2 tablespoons onion

3 sprigs cilantro

2 cups water

¾ teaspoon salt

To make the purée, combine all ingredients in a blender and blend until smooth. Transfer to a saucepan.

Add shrimp and heat over moderate heat until boiling. Remove from heat and add remaining ingredients. Enjoy! Serves 2.

Nate Mendel

One thing is certain: Nate Mendel knows his way around, has his priorities in order, and knows what makes him feel good. His favorite albums are *Jesus Christ Superstar* and *Hot Rocks*; his hobbies ("Golf does not count") include watching sitcoms and nature shows, and second guessing; "playing bass" is just his job. If he didn't tour with the Foos, Nate claims, "I'd be a journalist."

Though he believes he is the unknown member of the Foo Fighters "because I have boring hair," Nate, along with guitarist/vocalist Dave Grohl, is an original founding member of this all-the-rage alt-rock act (their 2002 release *One By One* went straight to #1) and the heartbeat of the band. He admits, "I bought my first bass not because I knew how to play one or had any intention of becoming a musician, but because I really wanted to be in a band and a friend had told me that the bass was the easiest instrument to play."

But what's *most* important, according to a friend, is that "Nate is a mellow cat who loves punk rock and snowboarding. He has a Devo tattoo on his leg and [also] plays in a great band called Sunny Day Real Estate. . . . He has [started] scoring films and seems to enjoy the challenges and opportunities that brings. He is a good friend, a great bass player, and an inspiration—and he rips on a snowboard, just pure athletic aestheticism."

Backstage with Nate Mendel . . .

If you were a food, what would you be?

Sugar.

What is your favorite food?

Fish, and specifically, the Tandoori Fish (which is salmon) from India's Oven on Beverly in Los Angeles. And Pop Tarts. I'm also a big fan of those sushi rolls with unagi and avocado.

Do you have a favorite restaurant?

The Bamboo Garden in Seattle is probably my favorite restaurant. It's kosher vegetarian Chinese food. The menu says that the recipes are derived from the kitchen of some emperor and are designed to be substituted for the meat dishes he was, for one reason or another, not able to eat during a certain time of the year. So although you're ordering the Almond Chicken, it's all vegetarian. Best thing to do is go during lunch and order the "C" special: corn soup, beef fried rice, spring roll, sautéed vegetables, and (best of all) sweet and sour chicken.

Do you have special "backstage food" requests?

Always hummus, fruit and vegetables for the juicer, and some kind of "fake" meat for sandwiches.

What music would you recommend to accompany your recipe?

"Skweetis" from the Melvins' *Stoner Witch* album.

Pea Soup

The greatness in this recipe is the Beau Monde and barley. If you don't like pea soup this one may be an exception (plus it's easy and lasts for a while).

2 quarts water

2 cups dry, split peas

1 cup celery, sliced

1 cup carrots, chopped

1 cup potato, diced

½ cup onion, diced

½ cup barley

¼ cup parsley, snipped

3 to 4 garlic cloves, minced

2 to 3 tablespoon Beau Monde

1 bay leaf

½ teaspoon dried oregano

1 teaspoon basil

1 teaspoon Italian seasoning

½ teaspoon salt

½ teaspoon celery seed

Pinch cayenne

Throw it all in there [a large pot], boil, then cover and simmer [over reduced heat] for an hour. Makes 6 to 8 servings.

Bob Kastelic

Get down with bluegrass band Moonlight Hoodoo Revue on a warm summer night or hot Sunday afternoon in the hills around Lake Tahoe in northern Nevada, and Bob Kastelic will do his magic—singin', pickin', and strumming his guitar and revving up the mood with fiddle in hand. And don't forget to bring a picnic blanket, a jug, and some favorite vittles and great homemade bread, compliments of Bob.

Backstage with Bob Kastelic . . .

If you were a food, what would you be?

Soup and bread are good together; I'd probably come back as them.

What is your favorite food?

Fresh, homemade bread!

Can you suggest a song to play while preparing this?

"Bad Moon Rising."

Basic Bread

6 cups lukewarm water

¾ cup sugar

3 tablespoons (about 3 packages) dry yeast

7 to 8 cups white or whole wheat flour (or any combination), divided

½ cup vegetable oil

2 tablespoons salt

In a large mixing bowl, dissolve yeast with sugar in the water. Add about 5 cups flour and beat [with a wooden mixing spoon] until the consistency of sloppy mud. Let sit for about 45 minutes, until mixture gets bubbly from the activity of the yeast.

Add vegetable oil and salt. Stir in remaining flour a bit at a time, mixing with a wooden spoon until it's too thick to mix. Turn out onto a floured board and knead in flour until dough is moist but not sticky.

Return dough to bowl, cover with towel to reduce drying, and let rise for an hour or so (if dough gets too big during that time, punch it down). At end of rising period, punch dough down as much as it goes.

Preheat oven to 350°F and grease six, 5 x 9-inch bread pans. Divide dough into six equal pieces (a sharp knife works well). Fold and roll each piece into a loaf shape and place in bread pans. Let rise for 30 minutes, then bake for about 30 minutes. (You might need to leave bread in oven for up to 45 minutes, depending on your oven: check that loaves have a golden brown color before removing from oven, rather than [baking for] the exact amount of time.)

Remove loaves from pans, let cool, then dig in. Loaves that won't be eaten right away can be frozen immediately and will seem nearly fresh when thawed later. Makes 6 loaves.

Tommy Aldridge

Tommy is revered as a drummer's drummer—a self-taught musician whose powerful technique lays down the hard-driving, solid, percussive foundation on which rock music is built. His compelling drum lines and dazzling solos have thrilled fans of Black Oak Arkansas, Pat Travers, Gary Moore, Ozzy Osbourne, and Whitesnake during the height of their success in the '80s.

To reciprocate the wealth of knowledge he has amassed as a professional musician, Tommy and a colleague pioneered "Rhythm Therapy," a way of helping people recuperate from physical injury through music. He also performs at drum clinics, teaching his art form to a new generation of drummers.

In 2003, their Silver Jubilee year, Tommy rejoined Whitesnake, wowing audiences once again with his trademark drum solo—torpedoing the sticks into the crowd halfway through his show and topping it off by performing with his *bare* hands!

Backstage with Tommy Aldridge . . .

If you were a food, what would you be?

Strawberry Twizzlers!

What is your favorite food?

Any breakfast food.

Do you have a favorite restaurant . . . Favorite item on the menu?

Genghis Cohen in Los Angeles, California . . . the Paper Chicken.

Do you have any special "backstage food" requests?

Fresh fruit.

What music would you recommend to accompany your recipe?

Music by a band called Depswa.

Potato Leek Soup

4 bunches of leeks (approximately), trimmed and chopped

⅛ to ¼ cup butter

6 cups chicken broth

3 pounds baking potatoes (approximately), peeled and cut into small cubes

Salt and white pepper to taste

Heavy cream

Trim the green off of the leeks, split them open to wash out any silt, and chop. Sauté the leeks in butter in a pot over medium heat for 5 to 10 minutes. Add the chicken broth, stir well, and add the potatoes. Reduce heat and bring to a simmer until the potatoes are tender, approximately 15 to 20 minutes. Season with salt and white pepper; stir in a dash of heavy cream at the last minute. Enjoy! Serves 4 to 6.

Gregg Bissonette

"It's one thing to play the music—it's another to translate the passion that's inside." Gregg's passionate powerhouse style, shaped by schooled technique, has been his ticket to musical adventures without boundaries.

A founding member of the David Lee Roth Band, Gregg has also worked with Santana, Enrique Iglesias, Joe Satriani, Maynard Ferguson, Bette Midler, and Don Henley, among many other top artists. His second album *Submarine*, which features a virtual "Who's Who" of guitar heroes, showcases his ability to "translate the passion" into many musical languages.

Whether he's keeping the beat with big-name bands or conducting clinics for budding drummers aged eight to eighty, Gregg notes, "I'm blessed to be making a living doing something I love."

Backstage with Gregg Bissonette . . .

What is your favorite food?

Indian food.

If you were a food, what would you be?

I'd like to be a strawberry, so I could spend my life in strawberry fields.

What song would you play while preparing this meal?

The song I would play while preparing this meal would be "Within You Without You" by the Beatles.

Curried Pumpkin Soup

There are so many great Indian recipes, but this is really easy to make.

1 large onion, chopped	2 cups pure canned pumpkin
¼ cup butter	2 cups heavy cream
1 teaspoon curry powder	1½ teaspoons salt
2½ cups broth (vegetable or chicken)	

Sauté onion in butter until golden brown. Add curry powder and cook for about 2 minutes, stirring constantly so the curry won't burn. Put onion-curry mixture into a food processor or blender and purée. Set aside.

In a large pot on the stove, stir broth, pumpkin, cream, and salt together. Add onion-curry purée to pot. Heat [over medium heat] and serve. Serves 4.

Rehearsal Notes

♪ Gregg notes: "Bolts brand [of curry powder] is good and available in hot or mild; you can find it at Indian grocery stores."

Reb Beach

A born musician, Reb Beach began playing piano and guitar at an early age without formal training. Later he attended the Berklee School of Music for a few semesters, but realized it was not for him and began recording his own music, a blend of jazz and rock called "fusion."

After winning a "Guitarist of the Year" contest with one of his fusion tapes, Reb headed for New York, where he became a hot session guitarist chosen by legends like Eric Clapton, Bob Dylan, and Roger Daltrey. He also met bassist and front man Kip Winger, and the two formed Winger, a hugely successful band that produced platinum albums and six Top 40 singles. Later Reb toured with Alice Cooper and Dokken, and in 2003 joined the guitar-driven band Whitesnake.

When not "plugged in" and entertaining the crowds with his electrifying, onstage energy, you'll find Reb cruising around on his skateboard, catching some rays at the pool, or simply enjoying an icy-cold Coors Light. (Go backstage with Reb on page 147.)

Spicy Chicken Wingers

I happen to be a lover of Buffalo chicken wings, and this is the authentic way they should be made. I hate when you go to [places] and you get these mushy giant wings soaked in hot sauce. It's just a mess. The key to good wings is the apple cider vinegar and the quick broiling at the end. Sometimes we have friends over for the football game and they think I am some kind of genius because of these little crunchy, spicy, gems. Enjoy!

3 pounds of chicken wings, cut at joints and grilled or deep-fried

2 tablespoons vegetable oil (if grilling) or 6 cups vegetable oil (if deep-frying)

½ stick (¼ cup) unsalted butter

3 to 4 tablespoons hot sauce such as Franks or Goya

1½ tablespoons cider vinegar (the key!)

Tabasco or ground red pepper to taste

To grill wings:

Preheat grill. Halve chicken wings at joint and pat wings dry. In a bowl, rub 2 tablespoons oil onto wings and season with salt. Grill wings on an oiled rack set 5 to 6 inches over glowing coals until cooked through and golden brown (8 to 10 minutes on each side).

To deep fry wings à la the Anchor Bar:

In a large (5- to 6-quart), deep, heavy kettle, heat 6 cups oil until a deep fat thermometer registers 380°F. Just before oil reaches 380°F, pat dry 6 or 7 wings.

Carefully lower wings into oil and fry, stirring occasionally, until cooked through, golden and crispy (5 to 8 minutes). With a slotted spoon, transfer wings to paper towels to drain. Pat and fry remaining wings in the same manner, returning oil to 380°F between batches.

In a large skillet, melt butter over moderately-low heat and stir in hot sauce, vinegar, and salt to taste (I double everything with the sauce). Add grilled or fried wings and toss to coat. Add a little Tabasco or ground red pepper to spice it up. Stick wings on a pan under the broiler for a little bit, to burn the sauce in there and make them crunchy. Serves 6 as an hors d'oeuvre or maybe 3 as a main course.

Chuck Bürgi

While growing up, Chuck Bürgi eagerly partook of the abundant musical banquet spread before him everywhere he turned—the appetizing stimulus of jazz, the blues that satisfied both soul and senses, the rich dessert array of rock 'n' roll. At home in every musical style, he has evolved into one of the most versatile and sought-after drummers in music today. Brand X to Hall & Oates, Rainbow to Meat Loaf, Blue Öyster Cult to Enrique Iglesias, he has played with them all.

In addition to recording and touring for myriad projects, this New Yorker also performed as a member of the Movin' Out Band in Billy Joel's Broadway play *Movin' Out*.

Backstage with Chuck Bürgi . . .

What is your favorite food?

Avocado.

If you were a food, what would you be?

A coconut.

Food for thought . . .

Cooking is like playing an instrument: you get out of it what you put into it.

What song would you suggest playing while eating (or preparing) this?

"Scenes from an Italian Restaurant" by Billy Joel.

Baked Stuffed Avocados

1 large onion, peeled and chopped

1 tablespoon butter or olive oil

3 large, ripe but firm avocados (not too soft)

1 cup walnuts, chopped

1 cup Gruyère cheese, diced

¼ cup Parmesan cheese, grated

2 tablespoons parsley, chopped

3 to 4 tablespoons sherry

Salt and pepper to taste

Preheat oven to 400°F. Sauté onion in butter or olive oil in a large skillet over medium heat until soft. Remove from heat and cool. Cut avocados in half, remove the pit, and scoop out avocado flesh carefully to avoid tearing the skins.

Dice avocado flesh and gently toss all ingredients together (if you over-toss you'll end up with guacamole!). Spoon a heaping mixture back into each skin, arrange in a baking dish, and bake for 7 to 8 minutes (or microwave on HIGH for approximately 2 minutes), until cheese melts. Season with salt and pepper according to taste. Enjoy! Makes 6 servings large enough to share.

Rehearsal Notes

♪ Feel free to substitute Monterey Jack or Cheddar cheese for the Gruyère.

Marco Mendoza

When asked to join a garage band in need of a bass player, fifteen-year-old Marco Mendoza, who had never touched a bass, jumped at the opportunity, telling them he could play. With his dad's help and encouragement, he picked up his first bass guitar for $8 at a local pawnshop.

Now an accomplished bass player and singer *par excellence*, Marco is regarded by many in the Los Angeles musical community as a master of his instrument. With his versatile style, flawless playing, and relentless drive, he has built a richly successful career anchoring the rhythm sections of a wide variety of bands including Thin Lizzy, Ted Nugent, and Whitesnake. Though soft-spoken in person, when the "Rudolph Valentino of Rock" straps on his bass, he captivates the audience with his exotic tattoos and engaging showmanship.

When at home Marco shifts gears and fronts the sizzling-hot Latin jazz trio Mendoza Heredia Neto. If you're lucky, you'll catch them playing on a Tuesday night at La Ve Lee, a favorite club on Ventura Boulevard in the San Fernando Valley (see All Access on page 269).

Backstage with Marco Mendoza . . .

If you were a food, what would you be?

Seafood or ceviche.

What is your favorite food?

Seafood.

Your favorite restaurant . . .

Teru Sushi in Studio City, California.

Special "backstage food" requests . . .

Fruit, fruit, and more fruit and an occasional energy drink.

Mama's Ceviche

This recipe has been in the family for generations; it was passed on to me by my mom, H.C. Ridley.

2 pounds white fish such as sole or red snapper (you can also use shrimp, lobster, crab, and scallops if you like the combo)

Lemon juice, freshly squeezed (enough to completely cover fish)

4 tomatoes, chopped

6 to 7 chiles (Mom prefers canned jalapeños), chopped

1 bunch green onions, chopped

1 bunch cilantro, chopped

7 garlic cloves, crushed and chopped

3 avocados, chopped

2 teaspoons oregano

Salt and pepper to taste

Cut fish into small pieces and place in medium size bowl. Then pour lemon juice over fish (cover fish completely). Set aside and let fish marinate in lemon juice for about 1 hour or until it changes to a white color.

While waiting for the fish, chop tomatoes, chiles, onions, cilantro, garlic, and avocado (you will add avocado just before serving).

Drain lemon juice from fish, add all ingredients including oregano and salt and pepper to taste, and mix. Each serving should be placed on a chilled leaf of lettuce. Presto ceviche! Enjoy! Serves 4.

Rehearsal Notes

♪ Add Tapatio hot sauce (usually found in the international food section of the grocery store) if you like to spice it up even more.

Chapter 2

Special Guest

Sizzlin' Sides and a Pasta Performance

Shania's Potato Roast—Shania Twain

Potatoes Gratin with Bacon, Arugula, and Caramelized Onions—Doug Aldrich

Green Tips Asparagus Vinaigrette with Poached Egg Mousseline— Chef Yves Gigot of La Ferme

Spanakopita—Timothy Drury

Donatella's Special Tuna Pasta—Leo Sayer

Joe's Italian Meat Sauce for Pasta—Joe Lynn Turner

Stevie's Meatballs—Steve Hamilton

Pasta Alle Bossi with Pizza Bread—Doug Bossi

Spicy Chicken Pasta—Eric Singer

Seared Tuna with Pasta—Peter Rivera

Linguine and Clams Castellamare—Frankie Banali

Shrimp with Pasta in Sour Cream and Tomato Sauce—Larry Hoppen

Shrimp Scampi Pasta—Joe Satriani

Pappardelle Genovese—Andy Hamilton

The "Sizzling Penne & Double Truffle" Blues Gratin—Adrian Vandenberg

Shania Twain

Seems like everything Shania touches turns to gold—or platinum. *The Woman in Me* soared to the pinnacle of the charts, and *Come On Over*, the most successful female solo artist album of all time, sold an astonishing 34 million copies worldwide. Refreshed and ready to rock from time spent with family (the Canadian-born singer calls both the Lake Geneva area of Switzerland and Northern Ontario home), there's an electric buzz coming from Shania when she recalls her single, "I'm Gonna Getcha Good!"

"There is a typical Shania attitude in the lyric," she says, "a definite female confidence. It's all about a girl who knows what she wants; she not only knows how to get it, but she's going to get it good."

Twain's international lifestyle seems to have opened her up to fresh innovation. On 1998's *Come On Over*, she mixed the album one way for the U.S.A. and another way for the overseas market. For her #1 hit *Up!*, she and "Mutt" Lange—husband, producer, and songwriting partner—achieved yet another level by recording three CDs with the same tracks but in completely different styles ("green" for country, "red" for pop), using different bands. But one fact remains unchanged: Shania has the same attitude, same unlimited horizons . . . and she's "gonna getcha good."

Backstage with Shania Twain . . .

What is your favorite food?

Anything vegetarian!

Can you suggest a song to play while preparing (or eating) this?

The soundtrack to *The Mission*.

Shania's Potato Roast

4 large potatoes (peeled or unpeeled)

3 to 4 garlic cloves, sliced into slivers

4 tablespoons olive oil

1 tablespoon dry parsley flakes

1 bay leaf

½ teaspoon salt

Sprinkle of pepper

4 tablespoons white cooking wine (optional)

1 teaspoon rosemary (optional)

Cut potatoes into quarters. Combine all ingredients (add the cooking wine and rosemary for variety) in a roasting pot or Dutch oven. Toss until potatoes are covered evenly. Place lid on pot and roast at 200°–250°F if you want it to roast slowly for a few hours (approximately 3 hours). If you "want it quick," roast at 450°F for 45 minutes. (Keep an eye on it in case your oven is really hot; it may cook even faster.) Stir it after 15 to 20 minutes into baking. Makes 4 to 6 servings.

Rehearsal Notes

♪ We found this to be a splendid "special guest" side dish when served with the Vinster Codzoni (recipe on page 114).

Doug Aldrich

Stacy Aldrich, wife of hot rock guitarist Doug Aldrich and owner of Seasons Catering in Los Angeles, shared this delectable dish with us. As a caterer, Stacy insists on using only the freshest ingredients and procuring seasonal produce from local farmers whenever possible.

When we served these "hot potatoes" at a holiday party, the *entire* table asked for the recipe! Her unabashedly taste-smitten husband informed us, "Stacy never ceases to amaze me with her creativity and originality in the kitchen. She can make [a] hamburger and French fries seem special." For more backstage dish on Doug Aldrich, see page 9.

Potatoes Gratin with Bacon, Arugula, and Caramelized Onions

12 ounces bacon slices, chopped

1 red onion, thinly sliced

2 tablespoons light brown sugar

1 tablespoon balsamic vinegar

2 cups whipping cream

1 cup whole milk

3½ pounds Yukon Gold potatoes, peeled, thinly sliced into rounds

1½ teaspoons salt

1 teaspoon freshly ground pepper

8 ounces arugula, trimmed, coarsely chopped, divided

2 cups Gruyère cheese, grated, divided

Preheat oven to 375°F. Butter a 13 x 9 x 2-inch baking dish.

Cook bacon in a large skillet over medium heat until crisp. Using slotted spoon, transfer bacon to paper towels to drain.

In same pan (pour out all but 2 tablespoons of bacon fat), sauté onions over medium-high heat until transparent, about 5 minutes. Add brown sugar and vinegar, continue to sauté for another 5 minutes. Remove from heat and let cool.

Mix whipping cream and milk in a bowl. In your prepared dish, layer one-third of the potatoes, slightly overlapping. Sprinkle with a little salt and pepper. Top potatoes with a thin layer of [approximately a third of] arugula, bacon, onions, and grated cheese. Pour ¾ cup of cream-milk mixture over potatoes and topping. Repeat layering process (I end up with 3 to 4 layers).

Bake gratin uncovered until potatoes are tender and cream mixture thickens, about 1 hour and 15 minutes. Let stand at room temperature for 15 minutes before serving. Makes 6 to 8 servings.

La Ferme

Nestled in the little picture-perfect town of Genoa—"Nevada's Hidden Paradise with People who Care"—is the historical "Pink House," home to one of the finest restaurants on God's green earth. Proprietors Gilles LaGourgue and Chef Yves Gigot have created an exquisite and comfortable French country dining experience: the atmosphere is inviting, warm, and intimate; the cuisine, creative and savory; and the food is prepared from the freshest ingredients (eggs are provided by the chickens—"les filles"—who live behind the house in the little barnyard). Many successful restaurant years in Beverly Hills and Incline Village, Nevada, have produced a *mélange* of photographs of luminaries, VIPs, and stars, adding a special charm to the décor.

Gilles' presence and *panache* are certainly key ingredients in this culinary gem. Animated and entertaining, he eagerly attends to the desires of each visitor. Whether happily introducing you to his animals on *la ferme*, or seeing that Chef Gigot creates a favorite dish in your honor (the asparagus below simply captivated Whitesnake's David Coverdale), Gilles *will* weave his magic and you *will* come to call La Ferme your favorite restaurant.

Green Tips Asparagus Vinaigrette with Poached Egg Mousseline

Chef Yves Gigot of La Ferme

6 to 8 of the best, fresh-looking green-tip asparagus that you can find

2 fresh, organic farm eggs: 1 yolk; 1 whole egg

Freshly ground white pepper to taste

Kosher salt or sea salt to taste

1 tablespoon unsalted butter

Juice of one fresh lemon

1 teaspoon extra-virgin olive oil

1 tablespoon white vinegar

1 tablespoon house dressing

1 teaspoon fresh Italian parsley, chopped

1 teaspoon fresh chives, chopped

Let's go to the kitchen:

First, bring a pot with 1 gallon of water to a boil with 1 tablespoon salt.

On a chopping board, cut the foot of the asparagus to fit on a plate. Start peeling the asparagus about an inch from the tip and all the way to the bottoms. Cook them in the boiling water for about 5 minutes or until tender, refresh them in ice water until completely cold; dry and reserve.

In a smaller pot, bring about 4 cups water to a boil and add 1 tablespoon salt and the white vinegar; keep it on the side simmering. In a little sabayon copper pan, put 1 egg yolk, 1 pinch of salt, freshly ground white pepper,

2 tablespoons of water, and start beating it on medium heat until it is fluffy and has doubled in size. Then stir in the butter and the lemon juice to taste. [When] your mousseline sauce is done, keep it warm.

In a frying pan with the olive oil, add the cooked and dried asparagus, salt, and white pepper, and sauté it on medium heat. In a little pot with the vinegar, break the whole egg and poach for 3 minutes. On a warm plate, arrange your asparagus in a bunch and add the dressing over it with the parsley.

Remove and dry the [poached] egg on a cloth and gently put it over the asparagus. Cover it with the mousseline sauce and finish with the chives all around . . . voila! This is just for one person, David.

Rehearsal Notes

♪ Now, dessert! Enchanted by our first taste of La Ferme's crème brûlée, we have waited *years* for the recipe; turn to page 210 and enjoy. *Merci*, Gilles and Yves!

Timothy Drury

Timothy Drury got his big break when Don Henley hired him to play keyboards on his "End of the Innocence" tour in 1989 (he co-wrote Henley's single "That Made Me Stronger"). He has since shared his vocal, guitar, and keyboard gifts with the Eagles, Joe Walsh, Stevie Nicks, Sheryl Crow, Melissa Etheridge, Jewel, and many others, as well as completing a solo album. In 2003 Drury took the stage with Whitesnake, tickling the ivories for their 25th anniversary world tour.

When not on the road, he continues song-writing, producing, developing unknown artists, and writing for film and television. Timothy is also a gifted photographer, his work showcased in galleries nationwide and on his Web site. (See All Access on page 269.)

Backstage with Timothy Drury . . .

What is your favorite food?

Comfort food, baked things, dishes that warm your soul . . . usually Mediterranean.

If you were a food, what would you be?

Spanakopita—it's Greek and so am I.

Food for thought . . .

Music and food are two of the fundamental elements of having a life worth living. When you can share the two with people you love, the gods definitely smile down upon you.

Can you suggest songs to listen to while preparing this?

It takes a good long while to prepare, so I usually put five favorite discs on the carousel: *Beatles 1*, *Gypsy Kings*, Tom Waits' *Frank's Wild Years*, the soundtrack from *Shawshank Redemption*, Pat Metheny's *Missouri Sky*. These favorites change weekly!

Spanakopita

Dedicated to my grandmother, Anna

This is my mom's Spanakopita recipe, who got it from her mother, Anna (who is also the person who bought me my first piano and piano lessons, I might add). She was born on a Greek island, so it's very authentic; lots of work but quite addictive when it comes together nicely. In the Greek chapter of the Drury household, Spanakopita was a main course! In reality though, it is usually considered an appetizer (especially if phyllo dough is used instead of rolled-out dough; phyllo tends to make it a finger-snack kind of thing). I would say that the rolled-out dough version should be considered no less than a side dish, only if you promise not to tell my mom!

Dough

6 cups unbleached all-purpose flour

3 eggs

1½ tablespoons salt

1½ cups cold water (approximately)

Filling

Eight 8- to 10-ounce bags prewashed spinach, washed again and chopped

6 yellow onions, minced

1 bunch fresh dill, finely chopped

1 cup grated Parmesan cheese, divided

¾ pound Bulgarian feta cheese, crumbled

1 cup olive oil (approximately)

Salt and pepper to taste

To make the dough:

In a large mixing bowl, fold all ingredients together by hand, adding water gradually. (Texture and consistency should be right on the edge between wet and dry; the dough will have elasticity with the slightest touch of tackiness.) Form into two equal-sized balls and let settle in the bowl, covered with a towel, in the fridge for 2 hours.

To make the filling:

Boil the washed, chopped spinach in a big pot for 2 to 3 minutes; strain it well, pressing all excess water out. [At the same time in a different pot,] boil the minced yellow onions slightly for 3 to 5 minutes to take the edge off; strain well and transfer to a *big* pot that is thick enough so everything won't immediately burn and stick on the bottom. Brown onions over medium heat almost to the point of caramelizing, but don't overdo it. Add cooked spinach and fresh dill; mix well and cook over medium heat for a few more minutes.

Add [about ¾ cup] Parmesan cheese and mix some more. Add feta cheese at the end of the mixing process. Salt and pepper to taste. Turn off the heat, cover, and set aside.

Using some of the olive oil, coat the bottom and sides of a good-quality baking pan (the kind that you would use for lasagna—but not as deep, if that makes any sense—you know, the kind that is 2 to 3 inches deep), with your hand, but don't over-oil it. (See Rehearsal Notes following the recipes.)

On a *big*, well-floured board, roll out your first ball of dough—not too thick, not too thin—but definitely big enough to cover the bottom of the pan, the sides, and a little extra to hang over the sides. (This takes a few tries. Mom's is always perfect, but she's been making it for more than sixty years!) Roll up the dough onto the roller [rolling pin] and then just unroll it over the pan. (When you roll it out it may be *way bigger* than the pan; don't sweat it . . . better way too much than not enough.) Press the dough into the corners to make a nice flat bed for the filling. Cut away the excess [leaving an inch or two of dough to roll up with top layer].

Add the filling and sprinkle the remaining Parmesan cheese on top of spinach. Flatten out the mixture to give an even filling.

Roll out the top dough and lay it over the filling. Roll the "slack" of the bottom dough and the top dough together to seal up the "pie" with a nice, rolled-up edge around the top. (The edges get nice and crunchy when cooked properly, which complements the lovely, soft spinach cheesiness of the filling.)

Add oil to top of dough (don't overdo it!) and spread oil around with your hand. Carefully score (cut the tip of the uncooked pie) into good-sized squares with a really sharp knife (it's impossible to cut after it's cooked).

Cook at 350°–375°F for at least one hour (usually more—it's an intuitive thing) until quite golden brown. Check the bottom occasionally for overcooking (put foil under pan if the bottom starts to cook way faster than the top).

Let sit for a while before cutting and serving (it will be blazing hot for a long time). You will actually have to cut all the way through the bottom dough now to get nice, clean pieces, since we only cut the top before it was cooked. Enjoy! Makes 8 to 10 servings.

Rehearsal Notes

♪ Though a 9 x 12-inch household pan could work in a pinch, this recipe begs for its own larger (10 x 15-inch), very well-seasoned ("thick and patina'd") pan. Timothy's mother has used the same pan for forty-plus years . . . and it is one of the secrets to a perfect spanakopita.

♪ Chef Timothy adds, "You can use 6 to 8 bunches (8 to 10 ounces each) of fresh spinach, which is the ideal, but takes way longer to prepare. If you're game though, the results are better with fresh spinach as you can include some of the stalks (you know the part right near the root that starts to turn reddish). When this stuff cooks down and gets tender, it really adds to the overall flavor, but as I said, it takes way longer to clean and chop."

♪ You may also substitute another type of feta cheese in the recipe, but note: "Bulgarian is much creamier and tangier than Greek, French or domestic, which is a good thing!"

Leo Sayer

Born Gerard Hugh Sayer in May 1948 at Shoreham-by-Sea, Sussex, England, singer and songwriter Leo Sayer is celebrating more than thirty years at the top of his profession. His first musical success came in 1972 with the songwriting of Roger Daltrey's (of the Who) first solo album, followed with Leo's first solo album that featured the hit song, "The Show Must Go On."

The ensuing years brought hit after soft-rock hit, including "Long Tall Glasses," "When I Need You," and the Grammy-winning "You Make Me Feel Like Dancing" from the platinum selling *Endless Flight* album. Further chart success came from ten more albums, featuring hits as diverse and unique as "More Than I Can Say" and "Living in a Fantasy." In recent years, Leo has traveled around the globe performing his songs to sellout crowds and has prepared a new album titled *Live* for release in 2003.

Backstage with Leo Sayer . . .

If you were a food, what would you be?

A plate of nachos.

What is your favorite food?

A mix: Italian/Mexican/Sushi.

Do you have a favorite restaurant . . . Favorite fare?

London: Cibo—great Italian country cooking.

Los Angeles: Lucy's El Adobe—authentic Mexican . . . chicken enchiladas washed down by the perfect margarita.

Italy: Donatella's [his wife's] mother!

Do you have special "backstage food" requests?

I don't trust backstage food too much, but a good sushi gives me energy for the show.

Food for thought . . .

Just that good food makes you write great songs!

What music would you recommend to accompany this recipe?

Italian opera—Verdi.

Donatella's Special Tuna Pasta

I don't cook, but Dona [my wife] makes the most amazing Italian dishes when we're back at home (she's from Montepulciano in Tuscany). Funny thing is she does it all by feel. I've never ever seen her consult a recipe book or measure any additives to any meal, but her dishes are always perfectly prepared. She's the best chef I know! This is my favorite meal.

500 grams (approximately 1 pound) penne, rigate, or fusilli pasta

2 to 3 tablespoons olive oil

3 to 4 spring (green) onions, finely chopped

3 garlic cloves, finely chopped

1 handful of fresh parsley, finely chopped

A small piece of red chile pepper, finely chopped

Salt and pepper to taste

2 tins (14.5-ounce cans) Italian peeled plum tomatoes, seeds removed if possible

1 carrot, grated

Contents of one medium tin (6-ounce can) tuna steak (solid white albacore) in olive or sunflower oil

Cook your choice of pasta according to package directions until tender but still *al dente.*

While the pasta is cooking, sauté the onions, garlic, parsley, and red chile in olive oil in a medium-sized (12- to 14-inch) frying pan over low heat until the onions are tender. Add salt and pepper to taste. Add tomatoes and continue simmering. Add carrot and stir regularly for 10 minutes. Finally, add tuna and simmer for 5 minutes, stirring regularly.

When pasta is done, drain, mix back into the sauce, and serve. Delicious! Makes 4 servings.

All the best, Leo

Joe Lynn Turner

Already on his way to stardom after the 1977 release of *Fandango,* recorded by his own band Fandango, Joe Lynn Turner and his dynamic vocals were quickly getting noticed. It was the attention of Ritchie Blackmore that brought Joe the exposure and success he so richly deserved. Along with Blackmore and the band Rainbow (and subsequently with Deep Purple), JLT sang his way up the charts to a number of Top 10 and #1 singles.

Turner has continued to record critically acclaimed albums as a solo artist and has become one of the most sought-after session singers in the business, cowriting songs and supplying vocals on albums by artists ranging from Cher to Billy Joel. He continues to record, tour, and set the standard for singers of all ages.

Backstage with Joe Lynn Turner . . .

What is your favorite food?

Italian and Japanese.

If you were a food, what would you be?

Devil's food cake.

Do you have a favorite restaurant?

Shabu Tatsu in New York City. I love the Shabu Shabu and the Korean BBQ there. I also love their Pork Kim Chee Gyoza, and their dipping sauces are phenomenal!

Do you have special "backstage food" requests?

Assorted fruit.

What music would you recommend to accompany your recipe?

Frank Sinatra . . . Andrea Bocelli.

Joe's Italian Meat Sauce for Pasta

This recipe was handed down through the family. My mother made the sauce. She came from a small town, Positano near Naples, and my dad came from Rome or just outside the city. I have dozens of relatives, and every Sunday there was a big supper with pasta, wine, and other dishes of Italian flavor—a big get-together that always ended with singing and dancing. I think that's where I got my love of music. . . . My dad sang great!

2 tablespoons (approximately) olive oil

1 medium-large onion, diced

1 bulb of garlic (at least 10 cloves), diced

3 whole bay leaves (for flavor, not to eat)

4 to 5 spicy hot Italian sausage links

1 pound sirloin, chopped

Two 28-ounce cans of crushed tomatoes

Two 28-ounce cans of whole peeled tomatoes

One bunch fresh basil leaves, washed, with stems removed

In a large pot, combine olive oil (just enough to cover bottom of pot) and diced onion, garlic, and bay leaves. Let simmer over low heat, stirring often, until garlic and onion caramelize. (Do not burn the garlic, just caramelize it on low heat.) Once caramelized, mash onion and garlic.

Squeeze sausage meat out of link-skin and place into pot. Keep cutting up sausage meat with a knife. As it cooks, use a potato masher to mash into very small pieces, stirring often. Increase heat to medium until sausage meat is brown.

Place chopped sirloin into pot and keep cutting it up into small pieces, stirring often until sirloin meat is brown. Lower heat.

Drain excess oil (but not completely; leave a little for flavor). Add crushed tomatoes, stirring often over medium heat.

Place whole peeled tomatoes into food processor and blend until tomatoes are crushed but not too liquefied. Pour into pot, stirring often over medium heat. Bring pot of meat sauce to boil, lower heat, and let simmer for 1 to 2 hours. (For thicker sauce, do not cover pot.) After cooking, stir in bunch of fresh basil leaves to sauce. Serve over pasta. Makes enough sauce for 8 to 10 servings.

Rehearsal Notes

♪ Use more cans of tomatoes if more sauce is desired.

♪ Freeze extra sauce in airtight plastic containers. You can thaw the sauce and use it in the future.

♪ For all our vegetarian kitchen rockers out there, we are honored to share an excellent recipe given to us by Lisa Walker, Joe Lynn Turner's publicist. Lisa notes, "This is a very sweet, fresh-tomato-taste, thinner-than-normal sauce [from her 100 percent Italian nana] that is *very* low in saturated fat. It is *great* as a sparse, simple sauce over 'rich pasta' like ravioli (especially homemade) or tortellini. It is also a *great* sauce for bread dunking."

Nana Barnello's Marinara Sauce

2 tablespoons olive oil (maybe more but start with this)

1 large yellow or Vidalia onion (if in season), finely chopped

5 large cloves garlic, sliced into quarters (so pieces are bigger than onion pieces)

1 heaping tablespoon tomato paste, unseasoned

Two 14.5-ounce cans stewed tomatoes, unseasoned and unsalted

1 cup fresh basil, lightly chopped, divided

Salt and freshly ground pepper to taste

Parmesan cheese, coarsely grated

Warm olive oil in saucepan over medium heat. Add onions and garlic and sauté, adding more olive oil if you think you need to (when you begin to smell garlic to make sure the garlic does not burn). As the onions cook and caramelize, take toothpicks and remove garlic slices and discard. (If you are a garlic lover, chop a few slices up and return them back to the pan.)

In a blender, pulse the stewed tomatoes for only a few seconds. Once onion is cooked, stir in tomato paste mixture to thicken sauce, whisking it around a bit to break it up. Add the stewed tomatoes from the blender.

Simmer for at least 10 minutes (or more if you have time) over medium-low heat. About 2 to 3 minutes before serving, add about ¾ of fresh basil to sauce.

Add more salt and pepper, if desired. (The beauty of using salt-free tomatoes is that you have complete control over how much salt you want to use.)

Prepare pasta according to package directions. (The best "shapes" to enjoy [this sauce] with are penne, angel hair, thin spaghetti, mini rigatoni, rotelli; I do not recommend using linguine, regular spaghetti, or any long, thick pasta.) When serving, top pasta with more fresh basil and fresh Parmesan cheese. Makes up to 8 servings.

Steve Hamilton

With formal training in saxophone and composition at the Guildhall School of Music & Drama, Steve founded Honey Music Ltd. in the Soho district of London in 1998, specializing in original composition for television, film, and commercials. He has worked on worldwide campaigns for mega-clients including Coca-Cola, Schweppes, and BMW, and he wrote the score for the feature film *Partners in Action* directed by Sidney J. Furie. Among Steve's current projects is a feature film written and directed by Ben Mole.

Steve also toured with such artists as George Michael, Lionel Ritchie, and Smashmouth throughout the United States, United Kingdom, and Europe in the late '90s, including a performance at the Tibetan Freedom Festival in New York City.

Backstage with Steve Hamilton . . .

If you were a food, what would you be?
Runner bean.

What is your favorite food?
Seafood.

Favorite restaurant and item served there . . .
The Fruit de Mer at Bofinger in Paris.

Special "backstage food" request . . .
Sushi.

Music to accompany this meal . . .
Godfather theme tune by Nino Rota.

Stevie's Meatballs

Hope you like it. Love, Steve Hamilton

Sauce

1 cup extra-virgin olive oil, divided

2 large onions, finely chopped

1 whole garlic head, crushed

4 tins (14.5-ounce cans) tomatoes, chopped

Big bunch fresh basil, chopped

Meatballs

500 grams (just over 1 pound) pork, cut into cubes

250 grams (just over ½ pound) turkey, cut into cubes

⅓ loaf (approximately) of stale ciabbata bread

2 small egg yolks

1 small red chili pepper, seeded

2 teaspoons sea salt

1 teaspoon dried oregano

1 teaspoon ground cumin

Black pepper to taste

1 tablespoon flour

1 small pack of mozzarella cheese

More fresh basil, chopped

1 500-gram pack (approximately 1 pound) fresh spaghetti

Lots of good Chianti

In a heavy pan, fry onions in half of the olive oil over very low heat for about 10 minutes. Add garlic and cook for another 10 minutes until the mixture starts to dissolve (don't let it brown). Remove about a third of the onion mixture and allow it to cool in a bowl.

Add the chopped tomatoes to the remaining onions in the pan and simmer for about half an hour over low heat. Add a handful of basil, pulse the sauce for a few seconds using a hand blender, and put aside.

Put the pork, turkey, bread, egg yolks, chili, salt, oregano, cumin, and pepper into a food processor and whiz until the mixture is blended but still coarse in texture. [Remove to a large bowl] and fold in the cooled onion-garlic mixture. Form into small balls (the size of squash balls is good!) and dust with flour.

Gently fry the balls in the remainder of the oil just to evenly brown them. Place them in a deep oven dish and pour the tomato sauce to cover them. Roughly break up some mozzarella and place on top of the sauce.

Bake for about 50 minutes in a preheated oven at 190°C (375°F). Remove from oven and add a bunch of chopped basil. Cook the spaghetti for only a couple of minutes, pour into a large serving dish, and spoon the meatballs and sauce on top.

Serve with watercress and rocket salad, plenty of Chianti, and a good gangster film, preferably *Godfather 2.* Makes 4 to 6 servings.

Doug Bossi

Doug Bossi's earliest guitar memory took place in Madrid, Spain, when a local barber, who was also a great Flamenco guitarist, serenaded him while Bossi was visiting his childhood home. Though exposed primarily to classical music in his formative years (in hopes he would become a classical musician), the intriguing riffs of rock 'n' roll lured Doug to pick up the electric guitar and explore a completely different soul of sound.

An exceptionally talented Los Angeles-based musician, Bossi has recorded and toured with many international artists including the Mustard Seeds, Jennifer Paige, and Eikichi Yazawa. In 1998 he was asked to share his multi-faceted guitar and vocal talents on David Coverdale's solo album *Into the Light*, and proved so valuable that he also helped write and coproduce the album.

With his focus now on solo projects, Doug says, "What I love most about being able to create music is the fact that someone with a piece of wood and wires can somehow take those same twelve notes that Mozart and Beethoven used to move us, and create something magical that stands the test of time."

Backstage with Doug Bossi . . .

What is your favorite food?

Anything my wife makes!

If you were a food, what would you be?

Candy.

Do you have a favorite restaurant and favorite item on the menu?

Gardunos in New Mexico—the green hatch chile there is phenomenal.

Do you have any special "backstage food" requests?

Green M&Ms.

Can you suggest music to accompany this recipe?

Sinatra at the Sands. Yeah baby!

Food for thought . . .

Only a shameless plug for a thanks to David Coverdale for showing me the finer aspects of a variety of wines!

Pasta Alle Bossi with Pizza Bread

1 pound mostaccioli

One 8.5-ounce can artichoke hearts in water, drained and chopped

One 8-ounce jar sun-dried tomatoes (julienne if possible), marinated in olive oil and herbs

1 to 2 cups Kalamata olives, pitted and chopped

1 handful basil leaves, chopped, ripped, or lightly crushed

2 tablespoons sun-dried tomato pesto

Pinch of sea salt

Bring a large pot of water to a boil. As you are waiting for the water to boil, prepare the artichoke hearts, sun-dried tomatoes, and olives. Drain the water from the artichoke hearts and chop them coarsely. If the sun-dried tomatoes are already julienned, they are ready to go. If you are unable to buy them julienned, then pour the olive oil and herbs [from the jar] into your sauté pan, place your sun-dried tomatoes on a cutting board, and julienne them. (The reason I prefer the sun-dried tomatoes this way, is that the amount of oil in the jar is just perfect: not too much, not too little. It is usually already seasoned with garlic, oregano, and other Italian spices, so it saves having to do much in the way of seasoning.)

Take the Kalamata olives and drain them as well. If you are able to find them already pitted, that's great; then just chop them. If you can only find the olives with the pits, then you'll have to pit them first: place them on your cutting board and with the heel of your palm, just press each olive firmly—you'll be able to remove the pit very easily—and once you've removed all the pits, then chop. (Be aware that even the ones that are already pitted often have an occasional pit or pieces of pits; always check them—your dinner guests will thank you.)

Heat your sauté pan on low (you should already have your herbed olive oil from your jar of sun-dried tomatoes in the pan).

Add your prepped artichoke hearts, sun-dried tomatoes, and Kalamata olives. Keep on low heat (you don't ever want this to sizzle; you just want to heat up your ingredients to a nice warmth).

Once your water has come to a boil, add some sea salt and then add your mostaccioli.

Boil until *al dente* (approximately 10 to 12 minutes) and drain.

Once you've drained it, place the pasta into a [large] bowl. Add 2 tablespoons of sun-dried tomato pesto. (The reason for doing this is to add color and flavor to the actual pasta. I used to just make the pasta without adding this step, but I found that it wasn't as rich as I would have liked. I then experimented and was using a few tablespoons of a tomato paste concoction I made. That was very nice, but one day I came across sun-dried tomato pesto and that was it! It had a rich flavor and also added the color I was looking for to the mostaccioli.) Stir it well with a spoon to coat all of the mostaccioli.

At this point, I like to add the basil to my sauté pan. (The basil will turn black if cooked too long; it doesn't look very fresh or appetizing that way, so wait until the very end.) You may chop or rip the basil leaves; I find that lightly crushing the leaves brings out the wonderful flavor. Add the basil leaves to your sauté pan and stir around to incorporate the basil flavor to your other ingredients.

Remove your sauté pan from the heat, add the ingredients to your bowl of pasta, and stir to distribute the pasta and the ingredients nicely. I recommend serving with pizza bread (recipe follows Rehearsal Notes) and a nice garden salad. Enjoy! Feeds 4 to 6.

Rehearsal Notes

♪ Our chef adds, "If you would like to make a heartier version of this pasta, feel free to add grilled chicken or grilled shrimp. It is such a simple and fast dish to make, and anything you enjoy will just add to the deliciousness of the dish." And, "If you prefer to buy your sun-dried tomatoes dry and dehydrated, then you'll have to soak them in boiling water to rehydrate and add your own olive oil and herbs. You can julienne them while dry, then add some of the boiling pasta water to a bowl and [soak] the dried tomatoes; usually 5 minutes is enough. To your sauté pan, add a few tablespoons of olive oil and freshly minced garlic, oregano—whatever herbs you love the most."

Pizza Bread

One 1-pound loaf frozen bread dough, thawed (or if you have time, home-made pizza dough—recipe follows)

1 to 2 fresh tomatoes

8 to 10 basil leaves, ripped or chopped

3 tablespoons of your favorite Italian salad dressing

4 ounces "pizza cheese" (mozzarella), finely shredded

Preheat oven to 350°F. Lightly grease and flour a baking sheet. Stretch your bread dough gently to fit your baking sheet. Spoon several tablespoons of your favorite Italian dressing onto the dough.

Slice your tomatoes into 8 even slices and place them, evenly spaced, onto your dough. Sprinkle your basil leaves onto your tomatoes and dough. Take your pizza cheese and sprinkle it all over your dough, tomatoes, and basil until it's nicely covered.

Place in the oven for 20 to 30 minutes, until golden brown and bubbly. Slice into 8 equal pieces so that each piece has a tomato. Serve with your favorite pasta.

If you want to try your hand at a homemade pizza dough, here's an ego-friendly recipe for the pizza bread.

Easy Pizza Dough

1 cup unbleached white flour

⅓ cup hot water

2 tablespoons olive oil

Pinch of salt

Mix the dough ingredients together in a large bowl and knead for 5 minutes. Let rest 5 minutes before rolling out.

Eric Singer

If you had asked teen-aged heavy-metal fan Eric Singer, sitting in the front row at a Kiss concert, if he thought one day he would be their drummer, he would have said, "In my dreams!"

Well, Eric has lived that dream, backing not only Kiss but other huge name groups like Black Sabbath, Queen, and Alice Cooper. For fun, he formed his own L.A. band Glamnation, doing covers of the glam-rock bands of the '70s. And when others living the rock 'n' roll dream purchase their drum kits, who do you suppose stars in the instructional video?

Eric especially enjoys professional studio drumming, as it expands his musical horizons in every imaginable style. In the studio, as in the kitchen, Eric has a taste for "the spice of life."

Backstage with Eric Singer . . .

If you were a food, what would you be?
Sushi, because I can be very raw!

What is your favorite food?
Italian, Indian, and Thai.

Do you have a favorite restaurant?
Woo Lae Oak in Los Angeles. They have the best tiger shrimp (and the neat thing is you barbecue the food yourself—to your liking).

Do you have any special "backstage food" requests?
Sparkling water, fresh fruit, and Pedialite.

Food for thought . . .

Eat healthy; you are what you eat!

What music would you recommend to accompany your recipe?

Always listen to music that does not distract; something that makes cooking easier. Mozart is a great choice . . . keeps the atmosphere relaxed.

Spicy Chicken Pasta

This is a very quick and easy spicy dish that anyone (even me) can whip up!

8 ounces bow-tie pasta	Salt and black pepper to taste
2 tablespoons olive oil	One 8-ounce jar sun-dried tomatoes, drained
4 medium, boneless, skinless chicken breasts; cut into bite-sized pieces	One 6.5-ounce jar artichoke hearts, drained
½ cup minced onions	½ cup black olives
1 to 2 cloves garlic, minced	1 tomato, chopped (optional)
1 teaspoon cayenne pepper	Fresh lemon juice (optional)

Cook bow-tie pasta (or pasta of choice) according to package directions.

Cook chicken in olive oil in a frying pan over medium heat until lightly browned (4 to 5 minutes). Remove with a slotted spoon and set aside.

Add minced onions, garlic, cayenne pepper, black pepper (and any other spices you like), and cook until transparent.

Add pasta and cooked chicken along with ingredients of choice—sun-dried tomatoes, artichoke hearts, black olives, fresh tomato if using—to frying pan and continue stirring until ingredients are mixed well and heated through. If desired, add a dash of freshly squeezed lemon juice to add a little depth. Enjoy! Makes 4 servings.

Rehearsal Notes

♪ This recipe is so versatile that you can substitute different ingredients—corn, black beans, and even bell pepper—for a nice, colorfully tasteful variation. In fact, try tossing in 4 to 8 ounces of feta cheese right before serving for a flavor boost!

Peter Rivera

One of the first drummers to sing lead vocal, Peter Rivera *is* the sound of Rare Earth. Originally called the Sunliners, their penchant for jamming psychedelic versions of Motown tunes got them noticed on the Detroit band circuit and soon led to a contract (and a new name) with the legendary label.

Their formula took them to the heights of Top 10 success in the '70s, until eventually the stresses of the rock 'n' roll lifestyle caused Rare Earth to crumble in 1976. Peter withdrew from live performing for many years, reemerging in 1991 with three other classic rock veterans to form the Classic Rock All Stars, with whom he continues to tour.

Backstage with Peter Rivera . . .

If you were a food, what would you be?
A salmon.

What is your favorite food?
Any kind of chicken.

Do you have a favorite restaurant?
Not really, my wife is a gourmet cook and I am spoiled.

What music would you recommend playing to accompany your recipe?
"Sittin' on the Dock of the Bay."

Seared Tuna with Pasta

Living in the Northwest, we eat a lot of fresh fish. This tuna recipe is one of our favorites.

Two 6-ounce ahi tuna steaks

½ pound angel hair pasta (or Chinese rice vermicelli)

Marinade

2 tablespoons fresh lemon juice

2 tablespoons sesame oil

2 tablespoons soy sauce

1 teaspoon black pepper

Sesame seeds

Dressing

1 tablespoon honey

¼ cup rice wine vinegar

½ cup canola oil

½ cup sesame oil

Salt and pepper to taste

1 tablespoon cilantro, chopped

½ cup roasted peanuts, chopped

Vegetable Medley

2 tablespoons olive oil

½ cup yellow pepper, julienne

½ cup red bell pepper, julienne

½ cup red onions, chopped

½ cup carrots, julienne

2 cups Chinese cabbage, julienne

1 teaspoon garlic, chopped

To make the marinade:

Whisk lemon juice, sesame oil, soy sauce, and pepper in small bowl. Place tuna steaks in baking dish, pour marinade over it, and turn to coat. Sprinkle with sesame seeds. Cover and refrigerate for 1 to 3 hours, turning occasionally.
Prepare pasta according to package directions.

To make the dressing:

Combine honey and rice wine vinegar in a mixing bowl and whisk. Slowly add oils until dressing emulsifies. Season with salt and pepper and stir in cilantro. Mix dressing into pasta while still warm. Add chopped roasted peanuts.

To prepare the vegetable medley:

Heat olive oil over medium heat. Add the peppers and onions and season with salt and pepper. Cook for 2 minutes. Add the carrots and cabbage and cook another 2 minutes, stirring constantly. Stir in the garlic and then stir vegetables into pasta mixture.

To assemble the dish, sear tuna in a *very* hot iron skillet, no more than 2 minutes each side. Remove from pan and set aside. To serve, mound pasta into center of plate. Slice the tuna and lay around the pasta. Makes 2 servings.

Frankie Banali

With his straight-ahead playing and unmatched showmanship, Frankie Banali has always been in demand. Already a mainstay of the rock world, he became known to millions of people in 1983 when Quiet Riot took the world by storm.

Frankie has also played with Glenn Hughes, Wasp, Alex Massi, and a host of others, and has lent his talent to many tribute CDs as well as movie sound-tracks including *Footloose*.

Frankie is still recording and touring worldwide with Quiet Riot, much to the delight of his many fans.

Backstage with Frankie Banali . . .

If you were a food, what would you be?

Salami.

What is your favorite food?

Pasta! Pasta! Pasta!

Food for thought . . .

Cooking is very therapeutic. You start out with a plethora of ingredients, attempt to make the dish flavorful but simple. It takes preparation, concentration, and discipline, which take our mind away from the daily routines of life. When finished, you reward yourself and others with the fruits of your labor.

What music would you recommend to accompany your recipe?

While preparing: Giacomo Puccini's *Tosca* or Guiseppe Verdi's *Aida*. While eating: Tony Bennett! Tony Bennett! Tony Bennett!

Linguine and Clams Castellamare

This recipe was a favorite of my father—handed down by example—and originates from Castellamare del Golfo, Sicily.

8 tablespoons extra-virgin olive oil, divided

1 pound local, wild mushrooms, stems discarded (can substitute oyster mushrooms, shiitake, small portobellos)

8 large garlic cloves diced

Dried crushed red pepper, to taste

1 cup Pinot Grigio or other white wine

5 pounds clams (about 2 dozen littlenecks are best)

1 pound fresh linguine

Sea salt

Black pepper, coarsely ground

Romano cheese, grated

Heat 4 tablespoons of olive oil in a large, heavy pan over high heat. Add mushrooms and sauté until they begin to brown. Using a slotted or draining spoon, remove mushrooms to a plate.

Add remaining 4 tablespoons of olive oil and garlic to the pan. Sauté until garlic is soft, but not brown. Add the crushed red pepper, wine, and clams. Cover and cook until clams open up, roughly 6 to 8 minutes. (Throw out any clams that did not open during the cooking process . . . *Atsa no good!*)

While the clams are cooking, cook linguine in a large pot of salted, boiling water. (When cooking pasta, try not to overcook: pasta should be a little firm.) Drain pasta completely and place in a large bowl. Spoon mushrooms over the linguine, then top with the clam mixture. Season with salt, pepper, and an ample supply of grated Romano. Serves 4.

Larry Hoppen

If you've ever hummed along to "Dance with Me" or "Still the One," then you've flown on the magic carpet of "the voice of Orleans"—the uplifting tenor of Larry Hoppen. Beloved for soaring melodies and harmonies, depth of musicianship, and social conscience, Orleans is still breaking new ground together after thirty years, with all three surviving original members.

A superb multi-instrumentalist and song-writer as well as vocalist, Larry has also recorded with Graham Parker, Michael Franks, Lulu, Livingston Taylor, Blues Traveler, and many others, and he tours the world with *Voices of Classic Rock*. His 1996 *Looking for the Light*, Hoppen's first album outside of Orleans, benefits Sunshine for HIV Kids, a nonprofit he founded to help young people living with the AIDS virus.

Backstage with Larry Hoppen . . .

If you were a food, what would you be?

High-quality chocolate.

What is your favorite food?

Seafood of all kinds (except urchins).

Your favorite restaurant . . .

DePuy Canal House; it's in a 300-year-old building in High Falls, New York. John Novi always has something new and amazing to try.

Special "backstage food" requests . . .

Fresh lemons.

What music would you recommend to accompany your recipe?

Pavarotti is a good choice. I particularly like *Nessun Dorma*.

Shrimp with Pasta in Sour Cream and Tomato Sauce

⅔ cup extra-virgin olive oil (approximately)

6 to 8 cloves garlic, chopped however you like

1 pound of the freshest, biggest, sweetest shrimp you can find (here in Florida, it's the Gulf pink shrimp), peeled and deveined

½ cup sour cream (approximately)

2 beefsteak or 3 plum vine-ripe tomatoes, cut into medium pieces (do not drain)

Salt and pepper to taste

⅔ pound *fresh* linguine or fettuccine

Locatelli Romano cheese

In a large pan, heat olive oil over medium heat. Add garlic and cook until it is browned (don't burn unless you love burnt garlic!). Add the peeled and deveined shrimp and stir a bit. (If the shrimp turns anything but red and white you bought the wrong shrimp.)

Stir in enough sour cream to turn sauce a bit creamy but not thick. Add tomatoes and sauté just long enough for them to warm up (the sauce will turn pink, thinning from the tomato juice as you stir). Add pepper to taste, and salt too, but remember you're using Romano cheese so don't overdo the salt!

Take the pasta—which you have simultaneously boiled to *al dente* perfection, not a second more!—and pour in the entire shrimp-sauce mixture. Toss well. Each person can add Locatelli Romano cheese as they wish (use a table grater or pre-grate for use). As Joe Pesce says, "Voy-la!"

Serve with a salad and some bread (also forks). This recipe will make about 4 to 6 servings depending how hungry you are!

Joe Satriani

Joe Satriani—or Satch, as he is often called—is a self-taught guitar virtuoso who took up the instrument at age fourteen after hearing the great Jimi Hendrix. When his fingers merge with the strings, timeless magic flows forth. With each new album, Joe Satriani wins over new fans as well as musicians with his groundbreaking style and legendary sounds, always asking himself, "What can I do that I haven't done before?"

In addition to his many critically acclaimed solo albums, Satch has collaborated with other legends including Deep Purple, Mick Jagger, and G3, an instrumental ensemble featuring such luminaries as Steve Vai, Eric Johnson, and Kenny Wayne Shepherd.

He has always generously shared his tremendous love and knowledge of the guitar with those who express a passion to learn this most seductive of instruments, teaching some of the top rock guitar players of the '80s and '90s such as Steve Vai, Kirk Hammett (Metallica), Larry LaLonde (Primus), David Bryson (Counting Crows), and jazz fusion player Charlie Hunter.

Shrimp Scampi Pasta

This recipe is a combination of my father's and mother-in-law's, with a little twist here and there from me. Enjoy!

2 pounds large prawns, cleaned and deveined

½ cup olive oil

2 tablespoons butter

2 cloves garlic, chopped

1 bunch parsley, chopped

1 tablespoon dried chile flakes

1 teaspoon sugar

½ teaspoon salt

Clam juice (optional)

1 pound spaghetti

Parsley, as garnish

Parmesan cheese (optional)

Boil enough water to immerse the cleaned shrimp for no more than one minute. When the shrimp start to turn pink, drain and set aside.

Combine olive oil, butter, garlic, and parsley in a large saucepan. Sauté mixture until the slightest browning occurs. Add shrimp and sprinkle with chile flakes, sugar, and salt. Cook until a light crust of parsley and spices forms around the shrimp. Be careful not to overcook! [Remove the shrimp], set aside, and keep warm. (Check the sauce: A bit of clam juice may be added to the sauce to stretch it if necessary.)

Cook pasta according to package directions. After cooking the pasta, drain, and add the oil, butter, and spice mixture to taste. Dish out pasta and add cooked prawns. Add salt, to taste, if needed and sprinkle some fresh parsley on top (my wife, Rubina, likes to sprinkle a bit of Parmesan cheese on her pasta as well). This should serve 4 people if you add a dish or two of vegetables and some Italian bread.

Andy Hamilton

Andy Hamilton is a poster boy for the multimedia generation. Equally adept with every flavor of saxophone, with wind synthesizer and keyboards and a panoply of electronic gadgets, he has combined musical technique with modern technology on projects from traditional concert tours and rock recordings to movie scores, music videos, TV shows, and commercials, collaborating with artists such as Duran Duran, David Bowie, Paul McCartney, George Michael, Tina Turner, Jon Bon Jovi, Bob Geldof, and the Boomtown Rats. Andy pops up wherever you turn, from the Net Aid concert at Wembley Stadium to the set of *Saturday Night Live*.

Backstage with Andy Hamilton . . .

If you were a food, what would you be?

I don't think I much fancy being eaten by anything or anyone. . . .

What is your favorite food?

Dozens of oysters and barbecued sea bass.

Do you have a favorite restaurant?

Val D'Isere, Rue de Berry, Paris, where the oysters and bass are my favourite things on the menu.

Food for thought . . .

This is a recipe for a cozy Italian supper for two: a delicious seafood pasta followed by Tiramisu (see recipe on page 208). If hearts haven't been melted after the first course, the Tiramisu is guaranteed to do the trick (whatever trick you are trying to do, that is)! Music to accompany this meal would have to be "Kind of Blue" by Miles Davis.

Pappardelle Genovese

To be followed by Tiramisu, of course:

1 packet of seafood cocktail from the supermarket (frozen or fresh) containing prawns, squid, cuttlefish, cockles.

(Life is too short to prepare this yourself, though this ethos does not extend to the tomato sauce.)

Sauce

½ leek, sliced

2 tablespoons onions, finely chopped

1 tablespoon red pepper, chopped

A little red chile pepper

1 clove garlic, crushed

Extra-virgin olive oil

Butter

Fresh herbs—lemon thyme, rosemary, oregano, chervil and/or tarragon, and plenty of parsley

1 tin (14.5-ounce can) of good-quality chopped tomatoes

Tomato purée or sun-dried tomato purée

Salt and freshly milled black pepper

Glass red wine

Pappardelle (dried is fine)

Chopped parsley, as garnish

First, prepare the dessert the night before (see recipe on page 208).

The day before the meal you must make the tomato sauce. (If you buy a ready made one from the supermarket, you will be missing the point entirely.) In a good, deep frying pan, sweat half a sliced leek with onion, red pepper, a teaspoon of chopped, moderately hot red chile [pepper], and a large (fresh if you can get it) crushed garlic clove in some extra-virgin olive oil and a small knob of butter. Cook gently until soft and the house smells like an Italian restaurant.

Throw in a little lemon thyme (without the stalks), some rosemary needles, a few fresh oregano leaves if you can get them, or if not, a good pinch of the dried stuff (careful though, as dried oregano can be overpowering). In fact you can add in moderation any fresh herbs that take your fancy, especially chervil or a little tarragon, though I'd avoid sage.

Add a tin of tomatoes (they'll probably taste better than any fresh ones you can buy, but use a brand that says "chopped tomatoes in rich tomato juice"). Add a decent squirt of tomato purée or even better, a squirt of sun-dried tomato purée. Season with freshly milled salt and black pepper and add a slug of the red or white wine you were saving for tomorrow but which you've opened "just to make sure it's okay."

Cook this sauce with the lid off on the lowest heat possible for any [amount of time] up to a couple of hours, adding a little water from time to time to keep it liquid. Put a lid on it, let it cool down, and put it in the fridge overnight. Take the lid off it the next morning and have a smell; you will immediately appreciate the worth of yesterday's preparation. (If you finished the wine, take two Neurofen or aspirin and drink a pint of water.)

If you bought a frozen packet of seafood cocktail, take it out of the freezer and defrost it in the fridge.

On the night, cook just enough pasta for two according to the manufacturer's instructions. (Pappardelle is a thick, ribbon-type pasta that perfectly complements this sauce.) While the pasta is cooking, warm through the tomato sauce (which should not be too liquid—reduce it if it is). Check the seasoning and add the seafood mix during the final minutes just to heat it through.

Give the cat a plateful of the seafood mix and its juice (at the same time rekindling your relationship with the hitherto oft-neglected creature—not to mention giving it a break from cat food—and impressing your partner with your largesse. It also stops the cat from pestering you while you're eating).

Drizzle some extra-virgin olive oil over the drained pasta and toss with the seafood sauce.

Throw some chopped parsley over the dish and serve. Makes enough to satisfy two people.

Take the Tiramisu out of the fridge, dust with some chocolate powder—drinking chocolate is fine—and serve. (If you don't like this supper, you'll probably love Chris De Burgh).

Rehearsal Notes

♪ Our gourmand also serves up these deliciously seductive tips: "The most attractive thing about this meal (apart from the food itself) is that you prepare almost all of it the day before . . . in fact both dishes benefit greatly from being made in advance leaving you free on the night to strut authoritatively around the kitchen impressing your partner with your expansive knowledge of Italian wine while the meal almost appears from nowhere. You could drink white or red with this meal, preferably Italian: Pinot Grigio maybe, or a Chianti, nothing too heavy (just make sure your partner drinks more than you do)."

Adrian Vandenberg

Adrian is one of the Netherlands' better-known rock 'n' roll exports. After achieving commercial and critical success with his group Vandenberg, this versatile guitarist and acclaimed songwriter joined the successful international band Whitesnake. Wildly popular with his fans, Adrian is known for his warm and gregarious personality.

Less well known is his gift for cooking. A distinguished chef, Adrian delights those close to him with his culinary inspirations, and could easily have made cooking his primary career.

Adrian resides in Holland, where he stays busy in the studio creating songs for other artists, movies, and television, and in the kitchen creating masterpieces for those who share his passion for great food!

Backstage with Adrian Vandenberg . . .

If you were a food, what would you be?

I'd be a couch potato, deep-fried in olive oil.

What is your favorite food?

Italianfrenchindian sushi-rolls.

Do you have a favorite restaurant . . . Favorite item on the menu?

The three-Michelin-star restaurant Lameloise in Savigny/Beaune, France—even their napkins taste great. I usually go for their Menu Degustation in which the chef can go berserk and you get bits of everything (and *everything* is amazing).

Have you ever written a food-related song?

The Vandenberg hit song "Burning Heart," which could be about the heartburn you can get after "pigging out" too ambitiously.

Do you have special backstage food requests?

If possible sushi—light and tasty! I like to have the sake administered intravenously during the concert.

What music would you recommend to accompany your recipe?

While preparing this recipe, I like to play anything by Stevie Ray Vaughn and Double Truffle.

The "Sizzling Penne & Double Truffle" Blues Gratin

200 grams (7 ounces) macaroni, uncooked

500 milliliters (18 fluid ounces or approximately 2¼ cups) double or heavy cream

1 bottled truffle (about 30 grams or 1 ounce), finely diced with its juice

100 grams (4 ounces) Gruyère cheese, grated, divided

Pinch of grated nutmeg

Salt and freshly ground pepper to taste

30 grams (1 ounce or 2 tablespoons) butter, for greasing the dish

Cook the macaroni very *al dente* and preheat the grill (broiler) for 10 minutes.

To make the sauce, pour the cream into a saucepan set over low heat and reduce by half, until it covers the back of a spoon. Add the truffle with its juice and cook for another 2 or 3 minutes. Still over low heat, gently stir in the macaroni and half of the Gruyère. Season to taste with nutmeg, salt, and pepper and give the macaroni another bubble.

Grease a gratin dish with butter and pour in the macaroni mixture. Sprinkle the rest of the Gruyère over [the top]. Place the dish under the hot grill (broiler) until bubbling and golden. Serve piping hot! Serves 6.

Chapter 3

Headliner

Electrifying Entrées

Caramelised Halibut with Parmesan and Herb Gnocchi, Mousserons, and
Sweetcorn Velouté—*The Tea Room at The Clarence*

Seared Hawaiian Ahi with Japanese Salsa—*Croce's Restaurant*

Grilled Sea Bass—*Doug "Cosmo" Clifford*

Ginger–Lime–Cilantro Marinade with Halibut—*Chef Colby Leonard for Mike Love*

Vinster Codzoni—*Vinnie Pantaleoni*

Zen Master DJ Mix—*Max Volume*

Whole Fresh Salmon à la Chinese Style—*Tony Hadley*

Ty Peanut Sauce with Rice and Veggies—*Tyler Haugum*

Not My Curry Recipe—*John Wesley Harding*

Chicken Saltimbocca—*Patti Russo*

Chicken Escalope with Cajun Mustard Sauce—*Paul Young*

Uncle Spikey's "Honeylamb" Chili—*Spike Edney*

Lamb Rogan Josh—*John Lodge*

John X's Big, Fat, Greek Leg of Lamb with Occasional Potato—*John X*

Veal with Lime Sauce—*Reb Beach*

Chile Maple Glazed Pork Tenderloin with Braised Red Cabbage and Sweet
Potato Purée—*Joey Altman*

Derek's Burritos—*Derek Hilland*

Southern Sloppy Buffalo Burgers—Rickey Medlocke

Bul Kogi—Ben Fong-Torres

"Uncle Omar's Famous Cliff Sauce" with Flank Steak—Alex Ligertwood

Garlic Rubbed Rock & Roll Rib Steak—Charlie McGimsey

Filet Mignon with Tequila and Poblaño Chile Sauce—Brett Tuggle

Oven BBQ Brisket—Stan Harrison

Bubble Bean Piranha à la Colorado Moose—Ted Nugent

The Tea Room at The Clarence

Undoubtedly the most talked-about award-winning restaurant in Dublin, The Tea Room at The Clarence Hotel features traditional dishes with a continental twist while offering friendly and flexible service to locals and hotel guests alike. Chef Antony Ely delivers an exciting style of cooking, using only the best, freshest Irish produce and changing the menu daily. Situated in the original south-facing dining room of the hotel, the restaurant occupies a light, spacious room with a soaring ceiling and double-height windows flooded with natural light. For dinner, The Tea Room takes on an understated, hushed elegance.

A part of the Dublin scene since 1852, The Clarence—situated in the heart of town overlooking the River Liffey and but a stone's throw away from the Guinness Brewery—was purchased in 1992 by two members of the rock group U2, Bono and The Edge. They took on the task of restoring The Clarence, creating their own vision of the ideal place to stay: elegant, refined, intimate. When you visit, it will be clear to you why *Travel & Leisure* remarked, "U2's Clarence Hotel has redefined Irish style."

Caramelised Halibut with Parmesan and Herb Gnocchi, Mousserons, and Sweetcorn Velouté

Four 175 gram (6-ounce) halibut steaks

Gnocchi

200 grams (7 ounces) baked potato, removed from skin

1 whole egg

70 grams (about ½ cup) strong (all-purpose) flour

35 grams (1¼ ounces) grated Parmesan cheese

1 packet (small bunch) parsley, finely chopped

1 packet (small bunch) chives, finely chopped

1 packet (small bunch) chervil, finely chopped

Salt and pepper to taste

Water for boiling

Oil for frying

Sweetcorn Velouté

½ onion, finely chopped

25 grams (about 2 tablespoons) butter, divided

200 grams (7 ounces or about 1½ cups) sweet corn, fresh or frozen

1 sprig thyme

1 clove garlic

200 milliliters (1 cup) water

100 milliliters (½ cup) milk

Salt and pepper to taste

Mushrooms

40 grams (about 3 tablespoons)
unsalted butter

200 grams (7 ounces) mousserons
or wild mushrooms

1 clove garlic, lightly crushed

2 sprigs thyme

Garnish

12 button onions, peeled

8 cloves garlic, skin on

100 grams (3½ ounces or 7
tablespoons) unsalted butter

20 grams (about 1½ tablespoons)
olive oil

1 packet (small bunch) fresh
spinach, washed

For the gnocchi:

Bake potatoes, allowing for shrinkage and skin. Remove the skin and while warm, add all other ingredients, mixing thoroughly. Roll on floured board and cut at 1-inch intervals. Then poach in salted [boiling] water [in a large pot] until they raise; remove to ice water. When cool, remove and dry. Fry gnocchi in a little oil until golden and keep warm.

For the sweetcorn velouté:

Sweat the onion in half the butter until soft, approximately 2 minutes. Add sweet corn, thyme, garlic, and water and reduce to approximately 50 milliliters (¼ cup) of liquid. Blend all together. Add milk and remaining butter. Keep warm. Whisk to serve.

For the mushrooms:

Heat a frying pan and add butter to melt. Then add rest of ingredients and simmer until soft. Remove from pan and keep warm.

To cook garnish:

In a frying pan, colour (cook until golden) button onions. Add knob of butter, season, and fry gently until soft, approximately 6 minutes. Place garlic into a small pan with [remaining] butter and pinch of salt and cook gently on stove until golden. Sauté in olive oil, season, and drain.

To prepare halibut and serve:

Preheat oven to 180°C/ gas mark 4 (about 350°F). Heat [ovenproof] frying pan. Add thin layer of vegetable oil and place halibut in pan. Colour for 3 minutes. Then place in oven for 2½ minutes. Remove from pan. Place spinach on plate surrounded by alternating gnocchi and mushrooms. Place fish on spinach, add garnish, and spoon the whisked velouté over the garnish. Makes 4 servings.

Croce's Restaurant

In 1968 Ingrid Croce and her husband, the legendary singer-songwriter Jim Croce, released their first album, *Jim and Ingrid Croce*. After Jim's untimely death in 1973, Ingrid pursued an independent music career until a series of vocal chord operations left her unable to sing. Having always enjoyed a feeling of extended family and the warm hospitality created by more than thirty-five years of cooking for family and friends, Ingrid opened Croce's Restaurant and Jazz Bar as a tribute to her late husband.

Her autobiographical cookbook, *Thyme in a Bottle: Memories and Recipes from Croce's Restaurant,* reflects an extraordinary life of travel, music, love, loss, adventure, and experience punctuated by the meals that nourished and encouraged her along the way. Her recipes are a collaboration of kind friends, generous chefs, and family traditions—there's a special dish that Ingrid would make for Arlo Guthrie when he came to visit—that have been enjoyed at Croce's and served in her own home . . . with love.

Seared Hawaiian Ahi with Japanese Salsa

Our Seared Ahi, from Thyme in a Bottle, is a signature dish here at Croce's.

2 pounds ahi tuna (sushi grade), cut into 6 portions

1 tablespoon cracked black peppercorns

Pinch of salt

2 tablespoons olive oil

½ cup shiitake mushrooms, sliced and stemmed

½ cup mushrooms (domestic), sliced

½ cup sherry

½ cup green onions, chopped

6 teaspoons pickled red ginger

1 cup Teriyaki Glaze (recipe follows)

1 cup Beurre Blanc (recipe follows)

½ cup Japanese vinaigrette

Salad greens

3 teaspoons white sesame seeds (optional, for garnish)

Season ahi with salt and cracked peppercorns. Place olive oil in sauté pan and heat over medium-high heat. Place ahi in heated oil and sear quickly until medium rare or to your liking (approximately 1 minute per side). Set ahi aside.

Put all mushrooms and sherry in sauté pan and reduce slightly. Add green onions, ginger, Teriyaki Glaze, and Beurre Blanc to the pan and cook until combined and slightly thickened, about 3 minutes. Do not heat too high (work with a medium-high flame).

Slice ahi into strips and put on a plate. Pour Japanese vinaigrette over greens and place in the center of the plate. Arrange ahi around greens and pour the mushroom sauce over the ahi strips. Garnish with sesame seeds on top. Serves 6.

Teriyaki Glaze Base Sauce

6 tablespoons soy sauce

2 tablespoons brown sugar

2 teaspoons white sugar

6 tablespoons Japanese vinegar

3 tablespoons sake or sherry

2 garlic cloves, minced

1 teaspoon fresh ginger, minced

1 teaspoon arrowroot dissolved in
1 tablespoon of water

Combine soy sauce, brown and white sugar, Japanese vinegar, sake or sherry, garlic, and ginger in a heavy-bottomed sauce pot. Bring to a boil (the sauce will flame as the alcohol burns off). Reduce pot to a hard simmer and add arrowroot mixture. Simmer hard for 5 minutes more.

Beurre Blanc

1 cup white wine

1 tablespoon shallots, chopped

2 tablespoons rice vinegar

1 cup (2 sticks) unsalted butter, cut
into small pieces

Salt to taste

Combine wine, shallots, and rice vinegar in a small saucepan. Bring to a boil over medium-high heat. Continue boiling until 1 tablespoon of liquid remains. Lower heat and whisk in cold butter. When butter is completely incorporated, remove from heat and set aside. Makes 1 cup.

Doug "Cosmo" Clifford

There are but a handful of drummers in the rock world who can be identified by one name—Ringo, Charlie, Moonie, Cosmo. For well over thirty years, Rock and Roll Hall of Fame member Doug "Cosmo" Clifford has been "laying it down deep, fat, and swinging," providing the groove for all the great tracks that Creedence Clearwater Revival—CCR—recorded in the '60s and '70s.

Along with long-time band member Stu Cook, Cosmo formed Creedence Clearwater Revisited in 1995 to play live CCR hits—touchstones of a generation like "Proud Mary"—and their band has taken on a successful new life of its own. Revisited is now touring the world, performing up to 100 shows a year, and has released a double live album, *Recollection*, featuring classics like "Susie Q," "Born on the Bayou," "Bad Moon Rising," and "Who'll Stop the Rain."

One of the few genuine nice guys in the biz, Cosmo will take time from a hectic schedule to chat with fans, pose for pictures, sign autographs . . . and swap recipes. Claims Cosmo, "Cooking is a hobby; I *love* to cook."

Backstage with Cosmo . . .

If you were a food, what would you be?

An avocado.

What is your favorite food?

All kinds of seafood.

Do you have any special "backstage food" requests?

Fresh fruits and vegetables and fresh salsa.

What music do you recommend to accompany this recipe?

Classical music.

Grilled Sea Bass

2 good-sized pieces of Chilean sea bass (if there is concern about the overfishing of Chilean sea bass, this recipe works great with all white fish and even salmon)

Marinade

1 cup soy sauce

4 to 6 cloves of fresh garlic, minced

Fresh ginger to equal the amount of garlic

1 shot of rum

1 tablespoon honey

Fresh lime juice

Combine all ingredients and marinate fish 4 to 6 hours. Grill [over medium-high heat] for 3 to 4 minutes on each side. Serve. This dish blends well with wild or brown rice and grilled or steamed vegetables.

Rehearsal Notes

♪ If you are concerned about overfishing and want to know which fish to enjoy and what to avoid, the Monterey Bay Aquarium posts an updated and reliable advisory on the Web at *www.mbayaq.org/cr/seafoodwatch.asp.*

Mike Love

When not holding center stage as the lead singer of the Beach Boys—the quintessential surf-rock success of the last four decades—Mike Love lives in a literal state of "Good Vibrations" high on a hill with his wife and children, overlooking the unparalleled beauty of Lake Tahoe, the gem of the Sierra Nevada.

His secret to "peace in the fast lane": transcendental meditation. Ever since 1967, when he met Maharishi Mahesh Yogi during a Beach Boys rehearsal for a UNICEF benefit, Mike has embraced a dedicated practice of TM to create balance, focus, success, and happiness in his life.

Knowing that the joy of a great meal is also essential to the welfare of the body, mind, and soul, the Loves' personal chef extraordinaire, Colby Leonard, is in charge of keeping the feasts in paradise simple, natural, and effortless. Here Colby shares a secret:

In the kitchen with Chef Colby Leonard . . .

I came up with this recipe one day for Mike Love and his family and they were totally stoked. Since that day it has become a regular around the house. I go back and forth grilling and baking the fish. Both ways are excellent, but I prefer to grill it.

You could use the sauce on almost anything including tofu. The nice thing about it is that the marinade is really easy to make, so other than the marinating process it is fast to prepare. As far as wine goes I would recommend a nice chilled Chardonnay. This recipe is a favorite amongst the Love household; maybe it will be at yours as well. Enjoy!

Ginger-Lime-Cilantro Marinade with Halibut

7 tablespoons ginger, peeled and chopped (a spoon works well to peel)

½ cup tamari

¾ cup water

½ teaspoon cornstarch, dissolved in 1 tablespoon water

¼ teaspoon white vinegar

2 cloves garlic, crushed

½ cup cilantro, packed loosely

2 dried red chiles, crushed

1 tablespoon brown sugar

1 tablespoon lime juice

1½ pounds halibut

Combine all ingredients but the halibut in food processor or blender. I like to marinate the halibut overnight, but 1 to 2 hours is okay. This recipe yields 1½ cups of sauce.

If you are grilling the fish, warm the sauce in a pan until it thickens; if not, the oven will do it for you. And don't forget to think of something that you enjoy while preparing this—that makes it taste all that much better! Makes 4 servings.

Vinnie Pantaleoni

In Vinnie's thirty-year bass-playing and singing career, he has performed with some of the biggest names in the business. Vinnie recorded two albums with the very successful '80s band Steel Breeze, including the debut album that reached the Top 10 in 1982 with the catchy hit song, "You Don't Want Me Any More," and has toured and performed with such groups as the Who, Billy Squire, Hall & Oates, the Greg Kihn Band, Kansas, Joan Jett, Missing Persons, Robin Trower, and the Babys. Currently, Vinnie plays with the Michael Furlong Band based in Reno, Nevada, and also plays guitar with his two younger brothers in a hometown band called Faceless Rebel. Wherever Vinnie goes, he is noticed as a very humble, well-loved musician.

Backstage with Vinnie Pantaleoni . . .

If you were a food, what would you be?

Marlin; they're such beautiful fish.

What is your favorite food?

Seafood—lobster, scallops, king crab legs—sautéed in butter and garlic.

Food for thought . . .

"Metal" with nachos—can't beat it!

What music do you recommend to accompany your recipe?

Mozart's *Eine kleine Nachtmusik*—second movement—Romanze (Andante).

Vinster Codzoni

3 to 4 cod fillets (medium to large cuts)

Two 15-ounce cans premium stewed tomatoes

2 cups mozzarella cheese, grated

½ teaspoon paprika

Pepper to taste

¼ cup parsley, chopped

Salt to taste

Preheat oven to 350°F. In a 9 x 13-inch casserole dish, lay out cod fillets (medium to large cuts), longways, so as just to cover the bottom of the dish.

Then take two 15-ounce cans of premium stewed tomatoes, open, and pour them over the fillets (you might want to spread out the stewed tomatoes, to cover as much of the fillets as possible).

Grate 2 cups of mozzarella cheese and sprinkle over the entire dish. (There should be a blanket of cheese covering pretty much the whole sha-bang! Does this sound good, yet?)

Next, we add the spices: paprika, sprinkled lightly, to give the cheese blanket a copper color; pepper (and this is up to your own discretion); chopped parsley over the top of the entire dish (to give it a little pizazz!).

Place in oven and bake for approximately 35 to 40 minutes (or until the fish breaks apart with a fork, when you go to check it). Let casserole stand for 10 to 15 minutes (the longer the dish stands the thicker the sauce will be), then salt to your liking and serve with dry white wine of your choice. Well, there you have it. Hope you enjoy. Serves 4.

Max Volume

Max Volume, popular DJ and guitar-strumming troubadour, was "raised by wolves and schooled by cocktail waitresses" before being inducted into the Nevada Broadcasters' Hall of Fame and awarded the Congressional Meritorious Award for Service to the Community from Congressman Jim Gibbons in 2001.

Max has released three self-produced CDs— *Psycho Betty Barbecue*, *Written in Stone*, and *Tales of What's Left of the West*—and has opened for Edgar Winter, REO Speedwagon, War, Steve Morse, Shana Morrison (Van's daughter), and the Fabulous Thunderbirds. Max even convinced his friend David Coverdale of Whitesnake to record a sweet reading of "The Night Before Christmas" on the air one holiday. When in Reno, treat yourself to a feast of "air candy" on KOZZ 105.9 FM, "Reno's Classic Rock," and "Pure Rock" KDOT 104-DOT-5, compliments of Max.

On the Air with Max Volume . . .

If you were a food, what would you be?

A pizza, I'm very well rounded.

What is your favorite food?

Ahi tuna.

Do you have a favorite restaurant . . . Favorite items on the menu?

I like the Black Mushroom Chicken at Two Guys from Hong Kong, and the Ahi Tuna at Rapscallion is to die for. One should also have a Super Burrito at Super Burrito [all in Reno, Nevada].

Have you written/recorded a song with a food title or theme?

Yes, but it's a thinly veiled reference to oral sex.

Food for thought . . .

You are what you eat.

What song would you suggest playing while eating (or preparing) this?

I really enjoy the newest Beck CD *Sea Change* or maybe *Morning View* from Incubus.

Zen Master DJ Mix

1 cup brown rice

One 16-ounce bag frozen
vegetables (preferably the country
blend: carrots, corn, and green
beans)

A 1-pound salmon fillet

Lemon pepper

Lawry's Seasoned Salt

Sprinkle of thyme

Soy sauce to taste

Cook the brown rice, steam vegetables, and bake the salmon at 325°F for ½ hour
in a covered pan. Season with lemon pepper, seasoned salt, and thyme.

When all are done [cooking], mix in large bowl, crumbling the salmon. Sprinkle
with soy sauce to suit your taste. Serve in bowls. Yum-Yum Good! Pure Food,
Pure Power! Makes 2 servings.

Tony Hadley

The former lead singer for Spandau Ballet has a warm tenor voice filled with depth and character that enables it to be immediately identified. Who doesn't remember the hit song "True!"? "Ah . . . ahh . . . ahh . . . ahh . . . ahh . . . / I know this much is true!" Owing to their great songs, unique sound, and musical ability, Spandau Ballet shot to fame and achieved spectacular worldwide success, continuing to record until 1990.

With the disbanding of Spandau Ballet, Tony Hadley began his solo career, recording albums of covers and original songs and fulfilling his love of live performance in an orchestral tour of Europe with Joe Cocker, Paul Michiels, Dani Klein, and Guo Yue. He continues to record and tour as a solo artist.

Backstage with Tony Hadley . . .

If you were a food, what would you be?

A Brussels sprout!

What is your favorite food?

Indian and Indonesian.

Food for thought . . .

My wife's and my Mum's Sunday roasts are just fantastic!

Do you have a favorite restaurant and favorite items on the menu?

Los Manos in Antwerp has fantastic Spanish food and the wonderful Flaming Bastard—extremely alcoholic! Also, Casa Jacinto in Palma, Majorca, has great fish.

Special "backstage food" requests . . .?

M&Ms . . . but with the brown ones removed!

What music would you recommend to accompany your recipe?

Slave to Love by Bryan Ferry.

Whole Fresh Salmon à la Chinese Style

One 6-pound, whole, fresh salmon, head and bones removed

¾ cup soya (soy) sauce

1½ cups spring (green) onion, chopped

2 teaspoons ground ginger

2 to 3 garlic cloves, minced

1 to 2 crushed red chile peppers

You simply bake the salmon within the tin foil, covered with lots of soya sauce and stuffed with all the listed ingredients for approximately 45 minutes on gas setting 5 (about 350° to 365°F). Obviously, check it, and if cooked, leave foil open, sprinkle with more soya sauce, and crisp for about 10 minutes. With that done, you simply serve and enjoy a chile, ginger, garlic, soya-sauced bit of wonderful salmon. Serves 8.

Tyler Haugum

Drawing on the magic of guitar legend Jerry Garcia, the verve of rock wizard Keith Richard, and the depth and idiosyncratic style of folk-rock veteran Neil Young, singer and guitarist Tyler Haugum has created a self-styled universe of progressive jam-based rock with a strong undercurrent of psychedelic rhythm and blues tossed in for good measure.

Living the good life at Lake Tahoe in Nevada and expanding his skills and interests, Tyler, who is featured on the Blue Nectar Band debut CD, *Tahoe Blue*, now jams regularly with his own band, Feelin' Young, playing originals and his favorite "best of" covers. After the gig, catch him in the kitchen. . . .

Ty Peanut Sauce with Rice and Veggies

Rice-veggie-tofu medley

2 cups organic basmati rice

1 bunch organic broccoli, cut into small flowerets

2 organic zucchini, sliced

1 organic red onion, diced, divided equally

Entire bulb organic garlic, finely chopped, divided equally

One 14-ounce package organic extra-firm tofu, cubed

2 tablespoons organic olive oil

Organic peanut sauce

1 cup organic peanut butter

1 teaspoon Dave's Insanity Sauce

2 tablespoons organic tamari

2 cups organic coconut milk

10 fresh organic basil leaves, chopped

1 organic green bell pepper, sliced

2 tablespoons black pepper

Juice of 1 organic lemon

Lotta love

First, begin steaming your rice. . . . This takes the most time. Chop and prepare broccoli, zucchini, onion, and garlic. Cut tofu into 1-inch cubes. Steam broccoli and zucchini for 10 minutes, cover, and set aside.

Fire up the stove. On low heat, sauté half of the garlic and onion in olive oil for 5 minutes. Up the temperature to medium-high, add tofu, and cook till lightly browned on all sides. Set aside.

In a separate saucepan, add peanut butter, tamari, and Dave's Insanity Sauce (to order, call 800-758-0372 or visit *www.davesgourmet.com)*. Slowly stir in coconut milk at medium heat. Add remaining garlic and onion from veggie medley, fresh basil, and bell pepper to the sauce. Cook for only 5 minutes to prevent over-thickening.

Divide rice equally among plates and add steamed vegetables and tofu. Top with peanut sauce, then with freshly ground black pepper and lemon juice . . . Voila! Serves 4.

John Wesley Harding

What's not to like about John Wesley Harding? He's honest (his list of "People It's Not Cool to Like But I Do" include Al Stewart, Gordon Lightfoot, the Carpenters, Cat Stevens); he's British ("And, Baste My Steaming Puddings! I imagine there'll be a lot of food and a little yuletide cheer too"); and he's got a nicely twisted sense of humor (see his recipe that follows).

Born Wesley Harding Stace, in Hastings, East Sussex—a Libra—this modern day troubadour sings his truth, guitar in hand, pushing the boundaries of contemporary folk and pop/rock, receiving consistently good reviews. Offerings include *It Happened One Night, Here Comes the Groom,* and the more recent *Swings and Roundabouts* ("What you lose on the swings, you gain on the roundabouts"). And he tours regularly to stay attuned to a large loyal fan base. So, next time the Happy Curry Cooker's in your neighborhood, invite him 'round to try *your* curry.

Backstage with John Wesley Harding . . .

What is your favorite food?

My favorite food is Indian, almost certainly. And that is what my recipe will be.

Food for thought . . .

This recipe—one of the recipes that I can make from memory—comes with a preamble, just like one of my songs. It's [adapted] from the book that got me into cooking curries, *The Great Curries of India* by Camellia Panjabi. I saw a sample recipe from it in the *Observer*, the English newspaper I have been buying every Monday wherever I am in America for the last twelve years. The picture looked good, but then, those pictures always do. I tried it, anyway, and it was utterly fantastic, so, in a completely unprecedented moment in my culinary history, I sent off for the book.

Since then I have made many great curries from it—I am a very happy curry cooker. The great things about making curries are many and legion:

- They take a long time but you can listen to a lot of quality music while you're doing it.

- They smell fantastic.

- You get to grind spices together and actually feel like a bit of a chef.

- You get to buy stuff called *asafoetida* and *star anise*. Everybody knows the *green cardamom*, but here you get to run across the *black cardamom* too.

- Sometimes you get to cook them in oil, and grind them, or make a paste. And then there's the nan bread and the chutneys.

You can make this recipe with anything really—chicken, lamb, prawns—it doesn't matter. Other things to recommend:

1. Ghee (clarified butter)—better than oil, fun to have on your shelf (see recipe following)

2. Stirring everything endlessly. Apparently this is what reveals the flavour. It's also strangely therapeutic.

Oh, and I would like to mention the leaf that is called the Curry Leaf. It has a fantastic smell (nutty, spicy) when fresh and grows a handy, strange mold on it so you can tell when its day in your fridge is done. It is way better than the Bay Leaf, its nearest competitor. Anyway, here is the main dish. You can make "making it" take as long as you like and [use] as much chicken as you want; that's always how much I use! (I like it on the bone, but chunks are good too.) It freezes well. Yey.

Not My Curry Recipe

Oil (or preferably that ghee stuff)

1 large onion, finely chopped

2 garlic cloves, chopped

A "square inch" of chopped ginger

1 teaspoon coriander powder

1 pinch of turmeric

¼ teaspoon of garam masala (approximately)

¼ teaspoon paprika

1 cup water

2 tomatoes, chopped

1 to 2 pounds chicken (or whatever you like; thighs on the bone is the best, I think)

Water

Coriander

In a large pot, fry the onion in oil or preferably that ghee stuff, 'til brownish. Add chopped garlic cloves and ginger. Add coriander powder and stir. Add turmeric and garam masala and then paprika. Fry this. It starts to smell good.

Add a cup of water and cook 10 minutes (it reduces a little). Add chopped tomatoes and cook for 5 minutes. Put in chicken or whatever you like and some more water (but not too much) and boil it, 'til it looks like whatever-the-main-part-is looks done. Sprinkle with coriander.

With this, I recommend boiling potatoes, chopping them, then frying them in a large amount of garam masala, and any other spices you fancy that happen to be left around. Throw some cauliflower in there too. And have a nan bread (warm) and some raita (a refreshing curd cheese relish) on the side. Eat.

Then invite me 'round to try your curry. I grade harshly.

With very best wishes,

john wesley harding

Rehearsal Notes

♪ To make that "ghee stuff," simply melt unsalted butter over medium heat, then let stand for a few minutes, allowing the milk solids to settle. Skim the butterfat ("whey") from the top and strain the clear yellow liquid (also called "clarified or drawn butter") into a container.

Patti Russo

Patti Russo was blessed with a voice that has allowed her to sing her way into some of the more delicious experiences of her life. Since 1993, she has been the lead female vocalist for hard rock staple Meat Loaf—literally a "food" that rocks—and has performed with Bryan Ferry, Trans Siberian Orchestra, Steven Van Zandt, and the surviving members of Queen. Multifaceted as a songwriter and actress in addition to her vocal talent, Patti starred in the London production of *Notre Dame de Paris* and lent her beautiful voice to *The Grinch* soundtrack.

And Patti continues to live life lusciously. Between gigs and tours and singing her heart out, she knows what fine ingredients are necessary to stir up some fun and happiness. Simply said, "I love to cook, sing, and laugh! Take those ingredients and add a house full of friends and family and *now* you are living a full (pun-intended) life!"

Backstage with Patti Russo . . .

If you were a food, what would you be?

A hot pepper!

What is your favorite food?

I'll never pass up some hot chicken wings!

Do you have a favorite restaurant and a favorite item on the menu?

My family's home—it's *all* good!

Do you have any special "backstage food" requests?

Tabasco and red wine vinegar . . . oh, and good bread! Let me tell you, on more than one occasion, backstage food can be hazardous to your health!

What music would you recommend playing while preparing this dish?

Gypsy Kings Greatest Hits by the Gypsy Kings.

Chicken Saltimbocca

"Chicken Rock-een-Rolla"

Before I sent in this recipe, I had to actually make it again because I didn't know the exact measurements of the ingredients! A little of this . . . a little of that—that was the way I learned to cook.

2½ pounds chicken cutlets, sliced very thin (you will need them thin so they roll up easier)

¼ to ⅓ pound Swiss cheese, sliced

¼ to ⅓ pound prosciutto, sliced (you can also use American ham)

3 to 4 tablespoons olive oil

1 cup white wine (use a cup from the bottle that you *should* already have opened while preparing this dish!)

Salt and pepper to taste

Oil for cooking

Place a slice of cheese and a slice of the prosciutto on each chicken cutlet. Roll up and stake with a couple of toothpicks.

Heat oil [over medium-high heat] in a pan large enough to hold all the chicken. Lightly brown each side, adding a bit of wine as you are doing this. Cook for 5 to 7 minutes. Add remaining wine. Lower heat and cook for another 10 minutes. Add salt and pepper to taste. This will serve 4-ish people.

Paul Young

Paul Young possesses one of the most melodic soul voices of recent years. In the early '80s, his penetrating tenor animated the popular British band Q-Tips. After they disbanded, he went solo, capturing hearts with his rendition of the Marvin Gaye classic, "Wherever I Lay My Hat," which stayed at #1 most of that summer. With the hit song "Every Time You Go Away" on his second solo album, his star status was confirmed.

Paul then took some time off, putting together an informal group with a totally different style to play around London just for fun. Los Pacaminos (a phrase that actually means nothing but which sounded to the band members like "pack 'em in") transformed British pubs into South-of-the-Border haunts with their Tex-Mex/Southwestern country rock. In 2002 they released an album titled *Los Pacaminos* to rave reviews.

Backstage with Paul Young . . .

What is your favorite food?

Cajun/Mexican/Italian.

If you were a food, what would you be?

A mole sauce.

Do you have a favorite restaurant . . . Favorite item on the menu?

The Ivy in London for their Sticky Toffee Pudding and the Ivy in L.A. for their Soft-Shell Crab.

Do you have any special "backstage food" requests?

No, I can't eat before I go onstage.

Food for thought . . .

Next time you make a cooked breakfast [with bacon], slice a banana lengthways and fry it in the bacon fat. Lay it on top of the bacon next to your poached egg and beans on toast. Yummy!

Can you suggest music to accompany this recipe?

Mariachi Cobre—*Este Es Mi.*

Chicken Escalope with Cajun Mustard Sauce

This is [inspired by] a sauce from K-Paul, the most famous chef in Louisiana. It's so easy, but guys, the girls will think you're the Don Juan de Marco of the kitchen if you make this!

4 large chicken breasts, skinned and boned

2 eggs

2 tablespoons olive oil

½ cup natural bread crumbs (not golden)

½ cup Nut Roast Mix (from a health food store; see note following)

Cajun Mustard Sauce

½ cup heavy cream (U.K. chefs, read that as light whipping cream)

½ cup sour cream

6 tablespoons Creole (read "whole grain") mustard

2 teaspoons Worcestershire sauce

1½ teaspoons prepared (read "French") mustard

½ teaspoon salt

¼ teaspoon black pepper

¼ teaspoon white pepper

¼ teaspoon red (cayenne) pepper

A couple of pinches of dried basil leaves

OK, turn on oven to gas mark 7 (220°C or 425°F). With a kitchen bludgeon thing (to tenderize), beat the chicken breasts down so that they are fairly flat. In a sensible dish, break the two eggs and whisk them together. In another dish, mix the breadcrumbs and Nut Roast Mix together.

In a large frying pan, heat the olive oil on high heat. Dip the breasts first in the egg mixture both sides, then the bread crumb/nut mix on both sides. Place them in the frying pan—high heat—and fry for a couple of minutes each side (golden, not black, is best!).

Transfer them to a baking tray and put in the center of the oven for about 20 minutes.

This next bit is *so* easy: Put all the ingredients for the sauce in a saucepan and bring to boil over medium heat. Stir, turn down the heat, and simmer for about 15 minutes.

Check the breasts are done (knife through the center and look: Is it still pink?) If not, cook a little more, maybe on the top shelf. Place each chicken breast on the plate, spoon the mustard sauce (3 or 4 tablespoons) over the top, and serve with, say, sliced, fried courgettes, sliced, fried yellow squash, and sliced, steamed carrots just for color (read colour!). No potatoes, guys, the girls will thank you for it. Makes 4 servings.

White or red wine, shoes off, game of footsie under the table, you know the rest. . . .

Rehearsal Notes

♪ Granose Nut Roast Mix is a savoury, vegetable protein roast made of ground peanuts, oat flour, gluten, onion, hydrolized vegetable protein, mushroom, onion salt, peppers, mixed herbs. It is difficult to find in the States, but you can try your ordering luck at *www.goodnessdirect.co.uk* or ask your local specialty food store to carry it.

Spike Edney

British multi-instrumentalist Spike Edney is among the most admired, versatile, and well-liked session musicians in the business. Specializing in keyboards, guitar, and trombone, he enjoys an enviable choice of touring and recording with celebrated artists such as Eric Clapton, the Rolling Stones, Bon Jovi, the Brian May Band, Duran Duran, Peter Green, Ben E. King, and the renowned Queen, with whom he has played keyboards since 1984.

Spike has also organized charity and tribute concerts including the finale at *Party in the Park*, The Prince's Trust concert in July 2000, which boasted a live audience of 100,000 and a radio and TV audience of 120 million. His own S.A.S. Band (Spikey's All Stars) was formed in 1994 to play a one-off gig, but, bowing to demand, they are still going strong!

Backstage with Spike Edney . . .

If you were a food, what would you be?

A barbecued wild boar sandwich (a bit tough or chewy maybe, but worth it in the end!).

What is your favorite food?

Roast pork with cracklin' or rabbit stew.

Do you have a favorite restaurant . . . Favorite item on the menu?

Le Colombe D'or at St-Paul Du Vence near Cannes/Nice, France . . . Anything at all.

Do you have any special "backstage food" requests?

Steak and kidney pudding.

Food for thought . . .

Rabbit stew with dumplings is God's food. Try it in Ibiza; it's the islanders' favorite dish.

Can you suggest music to accompany this recipe?

The Mavericks, Raoul Malo, Texas Tornados, or the Gypsy Kings.

Uncle Spikey's "Honeylamb" Chili

Warning! . . . This chili is addictive, especially on cold winter days in front of a roaring fire!

2 white onions, chopped

4 tablespoons olive oil

500 grams (approximately
1 pound) fine lean lamb mince
(more if you want it real thick)

Six 400-gram (14.5-ounce) cans
tomatoes with herbs, garlic, or chili

Three 15-ounce cans kidney beans

2 cups tomato paste

1 each—red, green, and yellow—
bell peppers, chopped

4 garlic cloves, chopped

2 tablespoons cumin

2 tablespoons paprika

3 teaspoons onion powder

1½ teaspoons fresh basil, minced

1 teaspoon garlic powder

3 teaspoons honey

A pinch of salt (if *really* necessary,
but try this without it, you'll live
longer)

Garnishes:

Grated extra-mature Cheddar
cheese

finely chopped red onion

sliced ripe avocado

crème fraîche or sour cream

Lightly sauté the onions in olive oil in a large pot (I use a stainless steel pasta pot) over medium heat for 2 to 3 minutes. Add the mince. Stir until cooked light brown. Add tomatoes and kidney beans. Add all other ingredients (except honey) and stir. Add the honey last and use more or less according to taste. Simmer and occasionally stir for at least an hour, the longer the better (tastes even more fab the next day).

When serving, garnish with grated Cheddar cheese, let it start to melt, then sprinkle finely chopped red onion all over. Then lay some sliced avocado over it and finally dollop on some crème fraîche or sour cream, to taste (some people like the cream on first then the cheese, it's up to you).

Serve with hot garlic bread, hot pita bread, or a warm French baguette and a robust Chilean Merlot . . . Yum Yum, Pig's Bum!! (Don't forget to freeze some for later.) Feeds 6 to 8. Enjoy!

Love,

Uncle Spikey

John Lodge

John Lodge is bass player, singer, and songwriter for English rock legend the Moody Blues.

Introduced to rock 'n' roll via American artists in the '50s, the Birmingham schoolboy suffered an early musical setback when he was busted from music class to woodshop for not knowing Beethoven's birth date, but he persisted, playing in local bands and writing songs while completing his studies. In 1966 he joined friends in the recently formed Moody Blues.

Among his many Moodies hits are "Ride My See-Saw," "I'm Just a Singer (in a Rock 'n' Roll Band)," and "Sitting at the Wheel," and his ebullient personality has animated four decades of live performances, including countless benefit concerts. John's *joie de vivre* is also apparent in his appreciation of fine wines.

Backstage with John Lodge . . .

If you were a food, what would you be?

Not fish!

What is your favorite food?

Fish.

Do you have a favorite restaurant . . . Favorite item on the menu?

Sheekeys in London . . . Oysters followed by Baked Cod and Garlic Mash.

Do you have any special "backstage food" requests?

That occasionally they make my favourite curry: Lamb Rogan Josh.

What music would you recommend to accompany your recipe?

Niafunké by Ali Farka Toure. *Chants of India* by Ravi Shankar (this was produced by George Harrison).

Food for thought . . .

[I like] barbecues outside with a jukebox playing the classics.

Lamb Rogan Josh

We enjoy this both on tour and at home.

Leg of lamb, diced into cubes

1 jar of Rogan Josh curry paste (approximately 10 ounces or 283 grams)

2 carrots, roughly diced

1 onion, roughly diced

2 garlic cloves, crushed

2 tablespoons oil

One tin (14.5-ounce can) chopped tomatoes

Water

Salt and pepper to taste

Basmati rice, steamed

About 2 tablespoons coriander, chopped (in the USA, it's cilantro)

Mango chutney

Coat the cubes of lamb in a little of the Rogan Josh paste. [In a Dutch oven or very large saucepan], sauté carrots, onions, and garlic in the oil. Add remaining Rogan Josh paste and cook for 2 minutes.

Then, add the tin of chopped tomatoes and a little water, bring to a boil, and simmer.

In another pan, fry the lightly coated lamb in order to seal the meat, draining off any excess fat.

Add the lamb to the sauce, and simmer gently for about 2 hours until the lamb is tender.

Season to taste with a little salt and pepper.

Serve over Basmati rice, with freshly chopped coriander sprinkled on the top, and with Mango Chutney on the side. The lamb will serve 6 to 8 people; prepare the desired amount of rice accordingly (approximately 1 cup, cooked, per person.)

Rehearsal Notes

♪ You may be able to find Rogan Josh Indian curry paste at an international marketplace or Indian food specialty store.

John X

Welcome to the bright world of John X, born in Queens to a Greek Orthodox priest father, an artist mother, and four sisters who taught him the joys of dressing up.

Majoring in math and engineering at Carnegie-Mellon, he was introduced "one colorful evening" to the behind-the-scenes world of music radio, and his genie was out of the bottle. Within months, John was in Hollywood.

He has worked worldwide with the Rolling Stones, David Bowie, Bonnie Raitt, David Coverdale, and other stars, but always returns to the Happiest Place on Cahuenga where the Emmy-nominated producer-writer-mixer has recorded "95,897 rockers, 82,464 rappers, 43,979 actors simultaneously beginning and ending singing careers, and 35,002 chicks studio owners wanted to impress."

His strategy is "Disarm and conquer"; his tactics are outrageous outfits, laughter, karaoke, and cooking. "My friends only love me because I feed them," sighs John, "but I've come to terms with that."

Backstage with John X . . .

If you were a food, what would you be?

Something made at Willy Wonka's Candy Factory.

What is your favorite food?

Pretty girls.

Do you have a favorite restaurant . . . Favorite item on the menu?

It's called Ago in Los Angeles, California . . . I love the Lamb Chops and the Gnocchi in Alfredo Sauce.

Do you have any special "backstage food" requests?

Pretty girls.

What music would you recommend to accompany your recipe?

I would prepare it to traditional Greek music because it all fits together. One might serve it to Stravinsky's *Firebird Suite*.

Food for thought . . .

I love you all.

John X's Big, Fat, Greek Leg of Lamb with Occasional Potato

"Psito Arni Me Patates"

This is my all-time favorite for any holiday. Essentially, it's my mom's recipe, though I probably use a lot more garlic and red wine than she does. There is no actual "recipe" per se, so think of this as a guideline only. Even people who claim not to like eating lamb will end up begging for seconds and thirds. There are never any potatoes left, no matter how many I make.

For the lamb:

1 leg of lamb

3 to 5 cloves garlic, peeled and thinly sliced

5 tablespoons butter, melted

Juice of 1 to 2 lemons

Salt and pepper to taste

Oregano

At least 1 bottle of red wine (for "scientific" purposes)

As many potatoes (or sweet potatoes, even parsnips) as you want, sliced into 1-inch cubes

As many carrots as you want (I use at least 5 pounds), cubed

1 golden onion, peeled and chopped into chunks

2 to 3 cups water

Pinch of cinnamon

Preheat oven to 450°F for about 30 minutes. Wash leg of lamb thoroughly. Poke slits in the lamb with a sharp knife and insert the slices of garlic into the slits. Brush lamb with the melted butter and squeeze the lemon juice all over it. Season with salt, pepper, and a little oregano.

Place in oven in a roasting pan. Lower heat to 375°F and add liquid of choice (I use whatever red wine I'm sipping while I prepare the lamb). Bake for about 3 hours, basting the lamb occasionally.

For the potatoes:

Slice and chop the potatoes, carrots, onion, and whatever other vegetables you're using and throw them all into a pan of water. Sprinkle with salt, pepper, oregano, a tiny little pinch of cinnamon, and a half-glass of the red wine (don't drown them, but keep them moist while cooking).

I usually put the lamb directly on top the potatoes, so it drips onto them. Should take a couple of hours as well (375°F is usually fine). Usually, I overdo it and cook extra [root vegetables] in a separate pan (for the vegetarians). Makes 6 to 8 servings.

Reb Beach

To read more about Reb Beach and to sample his favorite recipe for Spicy Chicken Wingers, please flip to page 36.

Backstage with Reb Beach . . .

If you were a food, what would you be?

A New York slice [of pizza], unparalleled around the world as a food that is impossible to recreate—the secret is in the water—and possibly the most satisfying food in the world. It has bread, dairy, and fruit (tomato?) in one hot, foldable, crunchy triangle.

What is your favorite food?

#1: Would have to be my wife's Cast Iron Porterhouse. She caramelizes onions and mushrooms in butter, and adds a little red wine for a killer sauce. She serves it with twice-baked potatoes, fresh whole green beans, and popovers.

#2: My Chicken Wings.

#3: Raw, cold, ground sirloin on a saltine with Lawry's seasoning salt.

What is your favorite restaurant and favorite item on the menu?

The Shepherd's Pie at the Harp and Fiddle in my hometown of Pittsburgh.

Do you have any special "backstage food" requests?

My special request is always just one thing: Coors Light! (I eat at catering and rarely eat backstage food.) A common practice among miserly musician types is to request foods that can be heated up in the microwave on the bus: Ramen noodles in cups, little snap-top soups, and Chef Boyardee thingies. I knew a guy who lived on the backstage food; he would make sandwiches from the deli tray and wrap them, and take a bunch of cereal and fruit for his breakfast in the morning. At the end of the tour, he had saved $2,000 in *per diem*. I, of course, owed money at the end of the tour.

What music would you recommend to accompany your recipe?

Little Feat, *Waiting for Columbus*.

Food for thought . . .

Eating healthy on the road is next to impossible, especially in Europe. I live at McDonald's in Europe and Japan. If I'm at a restaurant I always order spaghetti, which is the same word in every language. I wanted eggs one morning and flapped my elbows while making rooster noises to the waiter. They brought out a Cornish game hen and looked at me like I was a stupid American.

Veal with Lime Sauce

"Veal à la Dick"

Reb's wife Debbie tells us, "This recipe was invented by Reb's father, Dick Beach (I know, sounds like a gay resort). This is what he called 'The Dish.' This is a delicious dish—it is hard to stop eating—and has been a family favorite for more than twenty years."

1 cup of flour

1 teaspoon Lawry's Seasoned Salt

Freshly ground black pepper, to taste

1 tablespoon olive oil

2 tablespoons unsalted butter

1 pound of veal, cut for scallopini (see note following)

1½ tablespoons flour

1 tablespoon butter, melted

1 to 1½ cans (14.5-ounce) beef broth

Juice from 1½ limes

1 pound spinach noodles, cooked

Olive oil

Parmesan cheese, freshly grated

Mix the flour with seasoned salt and black pepper and set aside. Heat the oil and butter in a large heavy skillet over medium-high heat. Dredge veal in flour mixture and shake off excess. Working in batches, add veal to skillet and lightly brown, about 2 minutes per side. Transfer veal to a platter; tent with foil to keep warm. Repeat with remaining veal, adding more oil and butter to skillet as necessary.

Deglaze pan with beef broth and lime juice, scraping up brown bits from the bottom of the skillet. Reduce heat to medium and simmer, reducing sauce slightly, for about 8 minutes.

Mix [1½ tablespoons] flour and the 1 tablespoon of melted butter in a small bowl to form a paste. Whisk into sauce. Simmer until sauce thickens, whisking occasionally. Taste sauce; if it is too tart, add more beef broth. Return veal to skillet and continue cooking for another 2 minutes.

Serve with spinach noodles tossed with olive oil and freshly grated Parmesan cheese. Serves 4.

Rehearsal Notes

♪ Veal cutlets, cut from the round of the leg or rib section, are usually sliced across the grain ½- to ¾-inch thick and often pounded.

Joey Altman

For more than a decade, Joey Altman has been at the forefront of the San Francisco culinary scene. Formerly the owner-chef for the award-winning restaurant Wild Hare, Altman now brings his bold, eclectic style of cooking to Food Network's *Appetite for Adventure*.

Along with co-host Tori Ritchie, Chef Joey is parachuting—and skydiving and deep-sea diving and kayaking—into the great outdoors and sampling gourmet food around the globe. Everywhere they touch down offers a new breathless, delicious adventure.

In his spare time, Altman teaches at cooking schools, consults for the restaurant industry, and, last, but never least, rocks in his Back Burner Blues Band (for more dish, check in with Joey on pages 19 and 188).

Chile Maple Glazed Pork Tenderloin

Six 8-ounce pieces of pork
tenderloin

Salt and pepper to taste

Chile Maple Glaze

1 cup maple syrup

1 tablespoon ginger, minced

½ tablespoon garlic, minced

¼ teaspoon chile flakes

½ cup veal stock

4 tablespoons butter

In a saucepan, over medium heat, reduce maple syrup, ginger, garlic, and chile flakes for the Chile Maple Glaze by half (be careful not to allow to boil over).

Preheat oven to 400°F. Sear pork tenderloin in a sauté pan and roast in a hot oven until medium rare (approximately 6 to 8 minutes; it needs to be at an internal temperature of 140°F). Then brush with glaze and cook another couple of minutes.

Transfer meat from the pan to a cutting board. Add the glaze to pan with veal stock and butter. Reduce until thickened and season with salt and pepper. Serve with Braised Red Cabbage and Sweet Potato Purée (recipes follow). Serves 6.

Braised Red Cabbage

½ cup smoked bacon, diced

1 red onion, diced small

1 head red cabbage, thinly sliced

1 cup red wine

½ cup red wine vinegar

4 tablespoons grapeseed oil

1 tablespoon brown sugar

Salt and pepper to taste

In a heavy-bottomed pot, warm the oil over medium heat. Add the bacon and onions and cook for 2 to 3 minutes. Add the rest of the ingredients and cover. Turn down the heat to low. Cook for 20 minutes, stirring every few minutes. When cabbage is tender, season with salt and pepper.

Sweet Potato Purée

4 tablespoons butter

1 pound sweet potatoes, peeled and diced large

1 yellow onion, sliced

2 tablespoons fresh ginger, minced

2 cups chicken stock

2 cups heavy cream

Salt and pepper to taste

Place all ingredients into a large pot and bring to a simmer; cook for 30 minutes. Strain off excess liquid, purée, and season.

Derek Hilland

Derek Hilland began playing the piano at age four, and his love for the instrument flowered into a fulfilling musical career.

Derek has brought his considerable vocal and keyboard talents to rock bands as diverse as Iron Butterfly, Whitesnake, and Rick Springfield with whom he regularly tours and records. Highly regarded throughout the music world, Derek cherry picks session work and touring gigs between time spent on the beach at his home in LA, sleeping in, and sitting behind his keyboards writing music.

Derek has a huge appetite for life . . . and food!

Backstage with Derek Hilland . . .

If you were a food, what would you be?

Pizza. . . . Everyone likes pizza!

What is your favorite food?

Pizza.

Do you have a favorite restaurant . . . Favorite items on the menu?

My favorite, local (Los Angeles, California) restaurant is Inn of the Seventh Ray in Topanga. It has a wonderful atmosphere in the evening. I usually order different things each time I go. I've never had anything that I didn't like there.

Do you have any special "backstage food" requests?

Lots of it! My other favorite restaurant is the catering room backstage on the Whitesnake tour. I usually ordered most of the items on the menu; that is why the catering girls called me "full menu!" Oh, how I miss them. . . .

Food for thought . . .

Well, they [food and music] are two of my three favorite things! When done well, they both bring a smile to my face. Anyone who I have worked with will tell you that I play much better after being properly fed!

What music would you recommend to accompany your recipe?

Anything by the Red Hot Chili Peppers.

Derek's Burritos

Not recommended before an early A.M. flight!

6 to 8 chicken breasts, skinned and deboned

3 green bell peppers, diced

6 green chile peppers, diced

1 onion, peeled and diced

Crushed red pepper

6 to 8 whole wheat tortillas

1 bunch of fresh cilantro, finely chopped

2 pounds Cheddar cheese, shredded

1 head of lettuce, chopped

Hot salsa (I am from New Mexico, after all)

Cut the chicken breasts into approximately 1-inch pieces and put in a *large* frying pan over medium heat. Cook the chicken until it is almost done.

Add green peppers, green chiles, and onion to chicken and turn down the heat to low. Season with crushed red pepper. Cook for another 10 to 15 minutes, stirring every few minutes.

Spoon over tortillas, add cilantro, cheese, lettuce, and salsa and roll into burritos. Turn off the phone and go to town! I don't recommend eating more than six burritos in one sitting for health reasons. Feeds one tall, skinny musician with a hollow leg for 2 days. Feeds 6 normal people.

Rickey Medlocke

A member of the legendary Southern rock band Lynyrd Skynyrd since its formation, Rickey first came to prominence with his own band Blackfoot, so named for his Native American heritage. Although he began with Lynyrd Skynyrd as a drummer and backing vocalist, Rickey soon came out from behind the drum kit to dazzle on guitar.

In addition to recording, writing, and touring with Skynyrd, Rickey has found time to pursue an acting career, appearing in two feature films and on an episode of CBS-TV's *Nash Bridges*.

Rickey, who is three-quarters Native American, first tasted buffalo meat while on tour with Blackfoot. Now, he always chooses it over beef.

Backstage with Rickey Medlocke . . .

If you were a food, what would you be?

I would be ice cream for the obvious reasons! What other food can be licked?

What is your favorite food?

I enjoy sushi a lot; also Spanish food . . . any of my mother's dishes . . . but I really have no *favorite*. . . .

What music do you recommend to accompany your recipe?

Something *hot!*

Southern Sloppy Buffalo Burgers

2 pounds ground buffalo meat

8 buns (not your own, store-bought)

1 pound Pepper Jack cheese, sliced

2 large tomatoes, sliced

2 large onions, sliced

One 15-ounce can of chili (no beans), warmed

2 to 3 cups coleslaw (either homemade or store-bought)

Garnishes to taste: lettuce (optional), mayonnaise, mustard

Make up burger patties and grill on open pit or home grill. Cook burgers as you like them. When they are done, make your burgers as you would any time you have them, except then add the cheese, tomato, onion, followed by the chili and then coleslaw [and lettuce, if using].

Put the mayo and mustard on and be prepared for it to be *soooooooo* good and "sloppy"—that's why they are named that. If you cannot find buffalo [your local butcher should be able to order it], lean burger meat will do, but take it from the Indian, go for the buffalo—less fat and more protein!

Ben Fong-Torres

You couldn't hope for a more upbeat, sane and dryly revealing observer of popular music's halcyon era.

—*Billboard* magazine

Ben Fong-Torres, who grew up working for a series of family-owned and other Chinese restaurants, escaped into rock 'n' roll and became a *Rolling Stone* writer and editor (and a rock DJ and karaoke enthusiast). He's chronicled his passion for food *and* music in several of his books, including *The Rice Room: Growing Up Chinese-American: From Number Two Son to Rock 'N' Roll, The Hits Just Keep on Coming: The History of Top 40 Radio,* and *Not Fade Away: A Backstage Pass to 20 Years of Rock & Roll.*

Though his wife Dianne got him back in the kitchen with a birthday gift of cooking lessons, Ben continues to write for a variety of magazines, ranging from *Parade* to *Gourmet*, and regularly writes "a casual column about my various misadventures" for *www.asianconnections.com.*

Off the record with Ben Fong-Torres . . .

If you were a food, what would you be?

I'd be a bag of mixed nuts. I'm lucky to have done a bit of everything: radio, TV, writing for newspapers and magazines, publishing a handful of books, doing onstage interviews, panels, and speeches, singing, and being a character in a major motion picture *(Almost Famous)*. The emphasis, for sure, is on the "nuts."

Favorite food . . .

Cassoulet . . . steak and taters . . . meatloaf . . . short ribs . . . almond duck and fried rice (also known as the Ben Special at Yet Wah on Diamond Heights in San Francisco).

Food for thought . . .

Food and music . . . like love and marriage, you can't have one without the other.

What songs do you recommend playing to accompanying your recipe?

Anything you like. I like Boz Scaggs (himself an accomplished cook), Los Super Seven, Love Psychedelico, Shelby Lynne, the Mavericks, "Memphis Soul Stew" by King Curtis, and, for this recipe, "Green Onions" by Booker T and the MGs.

Bul Kogi

À la my favorite cooking teacher, Connie McCole, Bul Kogi is a Korean dish, a simple, marinated beef that's perfect with a side of rice and salad or vegetables.

One 2-pound flank or velvet steak (best if partially frozen)

½ cup onion, chopped

4 cloves garlic, crushed

5 tablespoons soy sauce

5 tablespoons sesame oil

1 tablespoon sugar

1½ tablespoons crushed black pepper ("peppermill grind" is best)

3 tablespoons dry sherry

1 bunch green onions (including greens), sliced diagonally

2 to 3 tablespoons peanut oil

Trim the fat from the steak. Cut steak in half lengthwise, then slice each half, across the grain, in thin slices, about ¼-inch thick.

In a baking dish, combine the other ingredients (except the green onions and peanut oil). Mix the meat with the marinade, tossing to coat the slices. Marinate between 15 minutes and 2 hours.

In a wok or heavy skillet (but really, a wok is best), heat peanut oil over high heat and stir-fry the meat for about a minute. In the last 30 seconds or so, add the green onions. This is enough for 6 to 8 people, or 4 plus leftovers.

Alex Ligertwood

Growing up in Scotland, Alex had a passion for American music, especially Motown, R&B, and soul. He loved that it was raw and electric and didn't hold anything back—a good description of his own vocal style.

In the early '70s, Alex introduced his big, soulful voice as lead vocalist for the Jeff Beck Band, later working with Brian Auger's Oblivion Express, Auger's Jazz-Rock Unit, the Average White Band, Narada Michael Walden Band, and the David Sancious & Tone Band.

Alex is most recognized as a member of Santana; he has recorded and co-written eight Santana albums since joining the band in 1979. A perfect showcase for his vocal power is "Somewhere in Heaven" from the album *Milagro*.

Backstage with Alex Ligertwood . . .

If you were a food, what would you be?

A peach.

What is your favorite food?

Cajun.

Do you have a favorite restaurant . . . Favorite item on the menu?

Ivy at the Shore in Santa Monica, California . . . Black Pepper Louisiana Shrimp.

Do you have any special "backstage food" requests?

Anything but "yard bird" (chicken . . . we *always* get chicken at gigs!).

What music would you recommend playing to accompany this recipe?

Dr. John or the Neville Brothers.

"Uncle Omar's Famous Cliff Sauce" with Flank Steak

One 2- to 3-pound flank steak

½ stick (4 tablespoons) butter

1 tablespoon Worcestershire sauce

½ tablespoon soy sauce

1 round teaspoon dry mustard

1 teaspoon paprika

1 dash Creole seasoning

Dash garlic powder

Salt and pepper to taste

Separately cook flank steak prior to putting sauce into broiler. [You can broil the steak within 2 to 3 inches of heat—the hotter the better—about 5 minutes on one side and 4 minutes on the other; don't over cook or it will be tough.]

Melt butter onto an oven-safe platter and cover with all other ingredients. Broil until bubbling. Remove immediately. Slice steak into thin strips [across the grain] and put into sauce. Serve. Makes 6 servings.

Charlie McGimsey

Charlie has shared his exceptional drumming talents for more than fifteen years with such notable bands as Stoneground, Steel Breeze, Pride in Peril, and longtime friend Michael Furlong. He has played on many albums and movie soundtracks, including *Witchboard*, and has opened for Huey Lewis & The News, Sammy Hagar, Eddie Money, Starship, and Peter Frampton, to name but a few.

More recently Charlie has toured with popular tribute bands including *Salute to Rod Stewart*, headed by lookalike-soundalike Rob Hanna.

When not playing drums, Charlie enjoys cooking a variety of foods and savoring a fine glass of wine.

Backstage with Charlie McGimsey . . .

What is your favorite food?
Everything!

If you were a food, what would you be?
A strawberry.

What music do you suggest playing to accompany this?
Burn by Deep Purple.

Garlic Rubbed Rock & Roll Rib Steak

2 tablespoons olive oil

3 tablespoons coarse salt

6 tablespoons McCormick
Montreal Steak Seasoning

4 tablespoons dry thyme

4 tablespoons garlic, chopped

Four 10- to 12-ounce rib steaks, on
the bone

Combine the oil, salt, Montreal Steak Seasoning, dry thyme, and garlic in a small bowl. Using this dry rub to season the beef, brush or rub the steaks with the seasoning mix and let marinate at room temperature for 20 minutes.

Over a hot barbecue grill, or under an oven broiler that has been preheated for at least 20 minutes, cook the steaks on both sides to the desired doneness. (Generally, a steak of this size, cooked over a barbecue grill, will be medium rare within 8 to 10 minutes—4 minutes each side—with a blackened exterior and a warm pink interior.) Check for doneness by pressing gently with a cautious finger. I would serve this dish with garlic mashed potatoes and steamed asparagus. Serves 4.

Brett Tuggle

This multi-talented musician grew up saying, "I can do that!" A first-grader in Denver, Brett begged for lessons on the piano his mom brought home. He taught himself guitar and vocals after hearing the Beatles, and at age thirteen, smitten with surf music and the Detroit sound, drove a tractor on a Kansas farm to buy an organ.

A few local bands later, he was chosen to tour with Mitch Ryder and the Detroit Wheels. Brett's contemporary-edged classic rock "chops" have kept him busy ever since, recording and touring with legends like Rick Springfield, Three Dog Night, Steppenwolf, Fleetwood Mac, David Coverdale and Jimmy Page, and Chris Isaak.

Brett was also with the original David Lee Roth Band, cowriting several of Diamond Dave's best-known songs, including "Just Like Paradise."

Backstage with Brett Tuggle . . .

If you were a food, what would you be?

I would be a strawberry shortcake dessert: luscious fresh strawberries and soft moist cake—whipped cream is a must (and you know what can happen with whipped cream and a romantic setting). How can you go wrong?

What is your favorite food?

Mexican and Indian are my favorite, but great Italian is right up there. Yum.

Food for thought . . .

I think when people travel they should try different [local] foods—you can always get the same ol' same ol' back home—or how else will you discover something new you've never tasted?

Can you suggest a song to play while preparing (or eating) this?

Almost any Beatle's song will do nicely, but either the *Rubber Soul* or *Revolver* albums would be my picks.

Filet Mignon with Tequila and Poblaño Chile Sauce

Sauce

¼ pound fresh poblaño chiles (approximately 6 medium chiles)

1 small white onion, thinly sliced

½ stick (¾ cup) unsalted butter

1¾ cups chicken broth

4 ounces cream cheese, cut into pieces

½ teaspoon crumbled soft chicken bouillon cube

Salt to taste

Steaks

Four 1¼-inch thick beef tenderloin steaks (filets mignons)

Salt and pepper to taste

2 tablespoons vegetable oil

⅔ cups tequila (preferably amber)

Lay poblaños on their sides on racks of gas burners and turn flames on high (or put poblaños on rack of a broiler pan about 2 inches from heat). Roast poblaños, turning with tongs, until skins are blackened, for 7 to 10 minutes. Transfer to a bowl and let stand, covered, until cool enough to handle. Peel poblaños, halve lengthwise, discarding stems and seeds (and ribs if less heat is desired), and chop coarsely.

Cook onion in butter in a 12-inch heavy skillet over moderate heat, stirring, until softened, for 7 to 8 minutes. Add chicken broth and bring to a boil. Remove from heat.

In a blender, purée onion mixture with cream cheese and poblaños until smooth (use caution when blending hot liquids). Transfer purée to a large skillet, and simmer at a low boil over medium-high heat, stirring, until slightly thickened (about 5 minutes). Stir in crumbled bouillon cube and season to taste with salt. Transfer sauce to a serving bowl and keep warm, covered.

Pat steaks dry and season well with salt and pepper. Heat oil in large, clean skillet over moderately high heat until hot but *not* smoking; sear steaks 5 minutes on each side.

Remove skillet from heat. Add tequila and ignite it very carefully, shaking skillet until flames die down. Return to moderately high heat and simmer steaks for 2 to 4 minutes (for medium rare), uncovered, turning once.

Transfer steaks with tongs to a plate. Bring [remaining] tequila mixture in skillet to a boil for about 1 minute while scraping up brown bits, then stir it into the poblaño sauce. Serve steaks topped with sauce. Makes 4 servings.

Rehearsal Notes

♪ Sauce can be made 2 hours ahead and chilled, covered. Reheat before serving.

Stan Harrison

Though being from New Jersey is not as bad as people think, saxman Stan Harrison was thrilled to park his Camden cab and jump on the bus when Southside Johnny called him to tour with the Asbury Jukes, embarking on a musical career in which he has played with Diana Ross, David Bowie, Mick Jagger, the Talking Heads, Bruce Springsteen, and many others. Between gigs and time spent composing and arranging horn for television, film, and other projects, Stan also founded his own sax trio the Borneo Horns and recorded and launched a solo CD, *The Ties That Blind*.

There's lots of time for reading on a tour bus, and Stan is especially proud of knocking off Proust's *Remembrance of Things Past*. He cites sax greats John Coltrane, Cannonball Adderly, and Charles Parker as key influences, but is just as likely to find musical inspiration in a book, a painting . . . or perhaps a favorite food.

Backstage with Stan Harrison . . .

If you were a food, what would you be?

An oyster.

What is your favorite food?

The oyster.

Do you have a favorite restaurant . . . Favorite item on the menu?

Balthazar in New York City . . . The fresh seafood platter.

Do you have any special "backstage food" requests?

Whatever it is, make it fresh, skip the junk, and don't skimp on the wine.

Food for thought . . .

Most certainly. This questionnaire has been most difficult to complete: as a food addict who has toured all over the place, it was almost impossible to pick a favorite food or restaurant. So far as actually being a food, I would not presume to be the equal of an oyster but would rather consider it something to aspire to. Why? Simply because the oyster is unostentatious, simple yet complex, varied yet consistent, welcome in many situations yet requiring a certain sophistication to be appreciated at it's fullest . . . all in all, almost perfect.

What music would you recommend to accompany your recipe?

Your favorite blues.

Oven BBQ Brisket

This recipe is perfect for those of us who have little time to cook but can't stand take-out every night. It requires almost no preparation and very little attention while cooking.

One 3-pound brisket

12 ounces (1½ cups) BBQ sauce

12 ounces (1½ cups) chili sauce

One 15-ounce can fresh, whole cranberry sauce

½ cup brown sugar

Salt and pepper to taste

Cayenne pepper to taste

What do I do now? Mix ingredients together in a baking dish large enough to cover the brisket with the sauce, put in a 300°F preheated oven and start checking after 2½ hours. It could require 30 more minutes if your oven is not accurate. (If you don't mind an extra step, pan-brown the brisket in vegetable oil for 5 minutes on each side before covering with sauce and putting in the oven. This is not necessary, though; the idea is *simple* preparation.)

Finale: Put on serving platter for at least one hour, heat remaining sauce in a pot to reduce, then slice [steak] against the grain and start eating. Serves 6 to 8.

Rehearsal Notes

  ♪ Stan adds, "The quality of the sauces used will make or break the meal; I use Gates BBQ Sauce from Kansas City and often add extra chili powder to the sauce."

  ♪ And, "For those not familiar with the particular cut of meat, the brisket is found in the lower front area of the steer. The recipe will work with other cuts, but the cooking time will vary."

Ted Nugent

Nuge delivers what you crave!—if what you crave is heading out on a "Sunrize Safari," teaching your child outdoorsmanship at the Ted Nugent Kamp for Kids, or cooking up a good plate of Maple-Bourbon Wild Boar.

Oh yes, Ted's music. With over 30 million albums sold worldwide, you won't be disappointed with the Motor City madman's 2002 release. A review in *glammetal.com* comforts fans by promising, *"Craveman is his most aggressive and offensive release ever. And that in itself is quite a feat. Unlike some of his peers, Nugent hasn't resorted to an 'Unplugged evening with Theodore Nugent,' or any lame sell-out antics like that. Yeah, sure he has his love songs, but instead of boy meets girl, his are of the boy eats girl nature. . . . Thank God some things never change."*

Ted, who claims he "Rock 'n' Rolls approximately 6 months per year, hunts 6 months per year," also holds honors as being named Father of the Year at his children's school, is the editor/publisher of *Ted Nugent Adventure Outdoors* magazine, and has stretched his literary muscle again with his cookbook *Kill It & Grill It*, cowritten with his "Queen of the Forest," Shemane Nugent. And you thought he was just an average rock star.

Backstage with Ted . . .

What is your favorite food?

Dead stuff on the grill! Pure, natural, organic, fresh, protein-rich deer, elk, caribou, moose, buffalo, lion, bear, duck, goose, pheasant, quail, grouse, pigeon, dove, woodcock, squirrel, rabbit, muskrat, beaver . . . all the natural chow.

If you were a food, what would you be?

I'd be a pissed-off wild boar, taking the life of any hunter who dared mess with my girls!

Do you have a favorite restaurant . . . Favorite items on the menu?

Any commercial establishment would have a long way to go to provide the quality of food we are used to, but Ruth's Chris is as close as they come.

Have you written/recorded a song with a food theme or title?

From my new *SpitFire* CD, "Craveman" and "My Baby Likes My Butter on Her Gritz" says it all.

Do you have any special "backstage food" requirements?

No junk food and whatever my crew desires (but my hunting buddies bring me the good stuff).

Do you have a signature dish you like to cook or serve?

Tribe Nuge dines exclusively on the perfect food we kill ourselves, so we take ultra care and respect in the handling and preparation of each critter and meal. The ultimate food is venison backstrap, that scrumptious tenderloin from the backbone, sliced into ½-inch thick medallions and quick-singed over hot coals with a caress of garlic salt and pepper butter (recipe follows).

What song would you recommend playing while preparing this?

Since I've written the best dinner music of all times, "Stranglehold" or my new "My Baby Likes My Butter on Her Gritz" would be perfecto!

Bubble Bean Piranha à la Colorado Moose

This is it, folks! The chow the whole world has been waitin' for! Proven at the hands of the most voracious of camp hogs, this rib-stickin' slop is the ultimate in hunt camp fortification. As the primary mainstay at the Nugent Whackmaster Headquarters, many a hearty hunter has maintained the killer instinct by gettin' a belly full of my primo-extremo brew. First experimented with as early as 1968, the recipe has changed little over the years, but rather improved with the spirit of adventure.

1 pound ground venison (any)

2 green peppers, diced

2 red peppers, diced

1 large sweet onion, peeled and diced

1 large white onion, peeled and diced

1 bunch scallions, trimmed and diced

1 large bowl fresh mushrooms, diced

1 whole clove garlic, peeled and squashed

½ pound butter

1 large box Creamettes (elbow macaroni) or sea shells (shell pasta)

1 side deer backstrap, cut into bite-sized pieces

¼ cup olive oil

Splash of white vinegar

Cayenne pepper to taste

Mrs. Dash seasoning to taste

Brown the ground venison in a large skillet. Add half of the peppers, onions, scallions, and mushrooms to the browned meat. Add the garlic and butter to the browned meat and vegetables. Stir vigorously.

Boil the pasta [according to package directions] and drain.

In a separate skillet, singe the backstrap pieces in hot olive oil and white wine vinegar. Throw the whole load into a large pot on low heat, including the remaining raw vegetables. Season according to taste. Stir in small amounts of water to desired consistency, and let simmer over lowest heat all day.

Refrigerate [leftovers] overnight and reheat for days to come (it's best when 2 to 3 days old). Slop a load onto bread, mashed potatoes, rice, or serve by itself. Throw a log on the fire, kick back, relax, and swap hunting lies. Serves about 5 average folks or 2 major swine.

Chapter 4

Encore

Desserts Worthy of a Standing Ovation

My Mum's Blackberry Purée—Brian May

Currant Cake—Sarah McLachlan

Sticky Toffee Pudding Cake—Chef Eugene McCoy of McCoy's

Oozing Chocolate Soufflé Cake—Joey Altman

Meringue Torte—Jacqueline Pierce

Gaggie's White Potato Pie—Jon Butcher

Desdemona's Island Pie—The Inn of Imagination—Tribute to Jimmy Buffett

Mr. and Mrs. Steve Lukather's Cherry Cheesecake 2002—Steve Lukather

Sweet Lorraine's Chocolate Swirl Cheesecake—Kathi Kamen Goldmark

Chocolate Tofu Pudding—Lauren Broersma-Cutler

Tiramisu—Andy Hamilton

Crème de la Crème Brûlée—La Ferme—Tribute to Cream

Cherry Garcia Phish Food in One Sweet Whirled Rockin' Hot Fudge Sundae

Brian May

One of the major creative musical forces behind the supergroup Queen, Brian May helped change the face of melodic rock music. His innovative, fluid, and memorable guitar structures amaze and delight fans of rock music all over the world, and his unique harmonies make his playing immediately recognizable. Queen continues to be hailed as one of the greatest rock bands of all time by fans and critics worldwide.

Today Brian remains active in music with the Brian May Band, Brian's post-Queen solo venture, and can often be seen playing "The Red Special," his self-crafted custom guitar, which took him and his dad two years to make. He is also very involved with astronomy—his other love—often venturing off to dark, distant locations to view celestial wonders.

My Mum's Blackberry Purée

This is something very simple, yet to me, even now that I am (nearly) grown-up, this is still the most delicious substance known to man (and vegetarian, of course).

200 (approximately 5 pints) luscious, fat blackberries

1 teaspoon water

2 to 3 tablespoons sugar

2 Bramley's apples, peeled and chopped (optional)

My mum made it like this:

First, pick the blackberries while they are at their best, in late summer. Only use the ones that are ready to be picked (these are black all over, and come off the plant with only a gentle pull). Wear covering on the hands and arms—the bramble bushes are vicious! About 200 luscious, fat berries is a good number to make enough purée for two luxury helpings, or to store in the fridge, to sip at for treats over a week or so.

Put the blackberries in a pan with a teaspoon of water to get them started, and 2 or 3 tablespoons sugar (this is where it gets naughty), though you can adjust this amount of sweetening to taste.

Gently bring to boiling point, stirring with a wooden spoon (that you don't mind getting stained dark purple). Turn the flame to low and keep stirring and squashing the berries until the liquid becomes an even paste, not longer than 5 minutes or so, because vitamin C doesn't survive very long at 100°C (212°F).

Now if you have a couple of freshly scrumped Bramley's cooking apples, they could be chopped up and put in the pan with the berries, for an extra tang. But blackberries on their own give the purest flavor.

Remove the pan from the heat and pour into a metal sieve, over a glass or china bowl. Use the wooden spoon to churn the paste around, squashing the juice through and leaving the seeds behind.

The pure, red elixir can now be eaten or put in the fridge. It tastes really fabulous poured over ice cream, or the "Junket" my mum used to make (a kind of vanilla *blancmange*), or as a sauce for fresh fruits, or just spooned slowly into the mouth as a wicked pleasure. My daughter also enjoys the purée frozen into an ice lolly.

Warning: This stuff stains everything it touches (wear a napkin) and is very acidic (go gently if your stomach is sensitive). But the flavor—it's a killer—is guaranteed to blast your taste buds into space! Makes 2 "luxury helpings."

Sarah McLachlan

This passionately talented Nova Scotian singer-songwriter-guitarist-pianist has gained a devoted following among fans with her clever concoctions of folk-pop confection and *plenty* of hearty food for thought laced throughout her music. As the organizer of the Lilith Fair, a spectacularly successful road show of the late '90s that celebrated emerging women in music, Sarah set the stage for future greatness for herself and many other female performers.

In addition to one of her finest offerings, *Fumbling Toward Ecstasy* (which features a tribute to love's sweetness in "Ice Cream"), Sarah has outdone herself many times over with her tours, many singles, full-length releases, compilations—*Slowbrew, A Food for Thought, Brewed Awakening*, among others—videos, soundtracks, and even a poetic cookbook contribution, *Plenty.*

Backstage with Sarah . . .

I remember this as a Christmas cake—my mother started baking in October and went all out for Christmas. She, wanting to please everyone, made this cake especially for me, as it was the one Christmas cake that wasn't full of that nasty petrified fruit and nuts and booze, all of which I hated. I think it was a recipe that came down from my grandma, as did most of Mom's recipes. And with baking, as it is chemistry, the recipes were tried and true and unchanged.

It's quite a heavy cake full of molasses, and it reminds me of her and Christmas, watching her weave her magic in the kitchen.

It's something that I make now for friends as a housewarming or just a treat.

Currant Cake

½ cup cream or half-and-half

1 heaping tablespoon molasses

¾ cup butter

¾ cup Demerara (or dark brown) sugar

3 eggs

2 cups currants

2⅔ cups flour

2 teaspoons baking powder

¼ teaspoon salt

Preheat oven to 325°F. Heat the cream and mix in molasses. In a separate bowl, cream the butter until light and fluffy. Gradually add the sugar. Add the eggs, one at a time, beating well after each addition. Stir in the cream and molasses mixture, then add the currants.

Sift the dry ingredients together and add to the wet mixture. Pour into a greased loaf pan and bake for about 1 hour or until a knife inserted in the middle comes out clean. Serves 6 to 8.

McCoy's Restaurant

A charming stone house built in the early 1800s in Staddlebridge, North Yorkshire, England, is home to an inn and two lovely restaurants watched over by the McCoy Brothers. Upstairs is the Cleveland Tontine, an award-winning restaurant known for elegant fine dining. On the ground floor, overseen by brother Eugene, is McCoy's, a delightful family-style bistro and favorite watering hole for visiting rock nobility, including native son, David Coverdale.

No stranger to rock 'n' roll, Eugene McCoy once held center stage in the '60s as the singer for a popular, local soul group, The Elastic Band. Now a highly regarded chef and sommelier, Eugene frequently appears on national television and writes restaurant reviews and food features for scores of magazines and newspapers.

In McCoy's warm, sociable atmosphere, a good time is guaranteed on every level with Eugene as master of ceremonies. In the kitchen, creative head chef Marcus Bennett produces hearty food that pleases even the most discerning palate, and in the dining room, ebullient host Eugene has been known to make his guests laugh so hard their cheeks hurt! There is no better choice if you are looking to enjoy a rollicking night out with family and friends along with a splendid meal.

Sticky Toffee Pudding Cake

Chef Eugene McCoy

1 kilogram (about 2¼ pounds or 5½ cups) dates, pitted and chopped

6 teaspoons bicarbonate of soda (baking soda)

2½ pints (5 cups) hot water

4 teaspoons vanilla essence (extract)

¼ pint (½ cup) Camp coffee (see Rehearsal Notes following)

1½ pounds (3 cups) butter at room temperature

2½ pounds (5 cups) sugar

16 eggs

3 pounds (about 12 cups) self-rising flour

Put dates, bicarbonate of soda, and hot water in a bowl; add vanilla essence and Camp coffee. Leave to soak while making the cake mix.

In a very large bowl, cream butter and sugar together. Add eggs; fold in flour. Add date mix to cake mix and mix together.

Spoon [batter] into three greased, 10-inch cake tins. Bake in middle of oven at 110°C (225–230°F) for approximately 2 hours (but check after 1½ hours and every 15 minutes after that until firm to the touch and a skewer through the centre comes out clean). This is a moist cake though; it should be soft in the middle—bouncy, springy, sticky-ish. Keep testing; if [you] bugger it up, just buy a crème brûlée from Marks & Spencers. This should make approximately 3 cakes.

Rehearsal Notes

♪ This recipe makes enough Sticky Toffee Pudding to serve an entire rock band. We have had luck cutting the measurements in half (and it will still serve 8 to 12 people).

♪ As noted on their Web site: "Camp Coffee, a thick black coffee syrup from Scotland with a groovy logo, is a secret blend of sugar, water, coffee, and chicory and is, like revenge, best served cold. To order, visit *www.sybertooth.com/camp/* or check at your closest specialty food store."

♪ Let us add this ditty from the *Joy of Cooking* © 1931: "Many British or 'Imperial' units of measurement have the same names as United States units, but not all are identical. . . . Also, the variable sizes of the British teaspoon and tablespoon [create] a further problem. Confronted with [this] dilemma, a British friend laughed and told us that there were no standard [sizes]; her own teaspoons and tablespoons had been in the family since the fifteenth century and [seemed to] fit the family recipes perfectly." Good luck.

Joey Altman

Whether heating up center stage with the Back Burner Blues Band (see page 19) or taking a walk on the wild side of gourmet dining in his TV show *Appetite for Adventure* (more on page 151), Chef Joey Atman has a fine taste for the good things in life, like this dangerously delicious, oozing dessert.

Oozing Chocolate Soufflé Cake

12 ounces bittersweet chocolate

6 ounces (¾ cup) butter

¾ cup less a tablespoon sugar, divided in half

5 eggs, separated

Melt chocolate with butter over a double boiler. Spray one dozen 2½-inch stainless steel cake rings with vegetable oil spray and set on a flat baking tray with a square of parchment underneath each ring.

Whisk yokes with half of the sugar to a pale yellow. Whisk whites until they form a thick froth, then add remaining sugar and whip to soft peaks. Fold yolks into chocolate; then fold in whites. Fill the cake rings almost to the top and chill in the refrigerator for 1 hour.

Preheat oven to 400°F. Bake cakes for 8 minutes. Gently lift cakes off of sheet tray and place on plates, removing the parchment squares by sliding them out from under the cakes. With a small paring knife, cut around the inside edge of the ring to free the cake from the ring and carefully lift ring off.

Serve with a scoop of vanilla ice cream on the side. The cakes should be slightly runny in the center, hence the name Oozing Chocolate Cake. Makes 12 cakes.

Rehearsal Notes

♪ The stainless steel cake rings can be purchased through restaurant or bakery supply stores or at fine gourmet shops.

Jacqueline Pierce

Music has always been opera singer Jacqueline Pierce's dream, and she is living that dream to its fullest. This highly regarded mezzo-soprano has appeared as a soloist with the Metropolitan Opera, the New York Philharmonic, and the National Opera Company, among others. She has also organized many professional choral ensembles in New York City, and her acclaimed choral arrangements of works such as *Sweeney Todd*, with George Hearn and Patti LuPone, have been conducted by such podium giants as Zubin Mehta, Sir Colin David, Ricardo Muti, and Leonard Slatkin.

Jacqueline has served on the choral and special projects panels of the National Endowment for the Arts and other musical boards, and also shares her talents through lectures and her private voice studio.

Backstage with Jacqueline Pierce . . .

If you were a food, what would you be?

Chatteauneuf-du-Pape '59.

What is your favorite food?

Pecan Sandies.

Do you have a favorite restaurant . . . Favorite items on the menu?

Chanterelle, New York City, New York . . . Everything!

Do you have any special "backstage food" requests?

Water.

What music would you recommend to accompany your recipe?

Robert Shaw Chorale . . . *Irish Folk Songs*.

Meringue Torte

Meringues

6 egg whites at room temperature

2 teaspoons vanilla

½ teaspoon cream of tartar

Dash of salt

2 cups sugar

Filling and Frosting

2 cups whipping cream

Six ¾-ounce chocolate toffee bars,
crushed (Heath Bars or Callard &
Bowser Toffee)

Dash of salt

In a large mixing bowl, add vanilla, cream of tartar, and dash of salt to egg whites and beat to soft-peak stage. Gradually add sugar, beating to form soft peaks.

Preheat oven to 275°F. Cover two cookie sheets with plain, ungreased baking parchment paper. Draw a 9-inch circle on each paper and spread meringue evenly within circles.

Bake in a very slow oven for one hour. When done, turn off heat and let meringue shells "dry" in oven (door closed) for *at least* 2 hours.

Whip the cream in a large bowl until peaks form. Fold crushed candy (reserve a small amount for garnish) and salt into whipped cream. Spread one-third of the whipped cream between layers; frost top and sides with the rest. Chill overnight and let sit for one hour at room temperature before serving. Garnish with additional candy. Serves 6 to 8.

Jon Butcher

It is tough to be compared to Jimi Hendrix, but Grammy-nominated Jon Butcher has been—favorably. Opening for the J. Geils Band even before he had a recording contract, Jon has completed sixteen internationally acclaimed, self-titled CDs and toured the world five times.

A producer, consummate guitar player, singer, and songwriter, Jon now spends much of his time filling the demand for his music in the multimedia entertainment industry. A sampling of his extraordinary work can be heard in the Showtime production *Jimi Hendrix: The Movie.* You may catch an occasional live performance by Jon, but more likely you will hear him in your local movie theater or on your television set.

Backstage with Jon Butcher . . .

If you were a food, what would you be?
A carrot.

What is your favorite food?
Thanksgiving turkey with all the fixin's (including Gaggie's White Potato Pie)!

Do you have a favorite restaurant . . . Favorite item on the menu?
Chin Chin in Studio City, California . . . The Chinese Chicken Salad.

Do you have any special "backstage food" requests?

Sushi.

Food for thought . . .

This, my grandmother's recipe, is four-square tested. It's stood the test of time, refinement, and revisionist tastes (just think about the last time you even considered taking a bite of a Twinkie). In a multi-pie world, this pie can be trusted—the pie-eatin' goods. This pie means business, no foolin'. Try it, you'll like it.

What music would you recommend to accompany your recipe?

The music of Randy Newman.

Gaggie's White Potato Pie

In loving memory of my grandmother

2 unbaked pie crusts (recipe follows)

6 medium white potatoes, peeled, boiled, and cubed

1½ sticks (¾ cup) butter, softened

6 eggs, separated

One 8-ounce can evaporated milk, divided

3 cups white sugar

1 teaspoon salt

1 tablespoon lemon extract

1 teaspoon nutmeg

Make the dough first (recipe follows). Peel potatoes and boil in enough water to cover, until tender. Drain.

Preheat oven to 350°F. Cube potatoes and mix well (as if making mashed potatoes) with butter until blended. Separate eggs (reserve whites for later); add yolks to butter and potatoes. Mix until well blended. Add half of evaporated milk. Mix in sugar, salt, lemon extract, and nutmeg and mix well. Add remainder of evaporated milk and blend well.

Beat egg whites until soft peaks form. Gently fold egg whites in to potato mix. Pour into pie crusts and bake for 35 to 45 minutes or until center is firm to touch and [the pies are] a golden color. Makes 2 pies.

Rehearsal Notes

♪ You can run out and buy your favorite brand of unbaked pie crusts or you can take center stage with this tried-and-true, fail-safe pie dough recipe made from scratch. Gaggie would be proud. . . .

Double-Crust Perfect Pie Dough
From Food Men Love

2 cups unbleached flour	½ cup *cold* Crisco shortening
1¼ teaspoons salt	⅓ cup *cold* margarine or butter
¼ teaspoon baking powder	⅓ cup *ice* water

Blend together the dry ingredients. Cut in the shortening and margarine or butter with a fork or pastry cutter until you achieve a fine, crumbly texture.

Dribble cold water over the flour mixture and mix together. Form 2 dough balls. Using sweeping strokes from the center of the dough toward the outer edge on a well-floured, cool surface, roll one ball to a ⅛-inch thickness and line two 9- to 10-inch deep-dish glass or ceramic pie plates with the dough.

The Inn of Imagination
Tribute to Jimmy Buffett

You can't depend on your eyes when your imagination is out of focus.

—Mark Twain

Nestled in the historic section of Napa, California, The Inn of Imagination is a classic example of Spanish Revival architecture—high ceilings, oversized rooms, and luscious gardens—but walk inside and enter a unique and fanciful universe. You will find that each bed & breakfast room is dedicated to a celebrated "imagineer" and the spirit of that person is celebrated with period furniture, biographies, memorabilia, and collections of their work.

Our favorite room? The Jimmy Buffett Room, of course. As the tale goes, "Jimmy Buffett was born on Christmas day, 1946, and has been living his life like a gift ever since." His tropical folk-rock style endears him to millions of some of the most loyal fans in all of music.

Treat yourself to a stay in this room, and proprietor and "thinkster" Kim Thomas ensures that you will have the quintessential Parrothead experience with Desdemona as your guide. Desdemona, a character in Jimmy's books and several songs who runs the Bake Shop and Satellite Station on Boomtown, is depicted flying her rocket ship, the *Cosmic Muffin*, out to the Pleiades in a forty-foot mural on the ceiling of Jimmy's room at the inn. Margaritaville, here we come!

Desdemona's Island Pie

Crust

16 graham crackers, crushed

3 tablespoons granulated sugar

¼ cup butter, melted

Filling

4 extra large egg yolks

One 14-ounce can sweetened condensed milk

¼ cup fresh key lime juice, divided

¼ cup fresh Meyer lemon juice (do not use non-Meyer lemons), divided

1 teaspoon key lime peel, finely grated

1 teaspoon Meyer lemon peel, finely grated

Crème fraîche, for garnish

Make the pie crust first. Preheat oven to 350°F. Mix ingredients and line a 9-inch pie plate (be sure to press firmly into bottom and sides). Bake 8 to 10 minutes until light brown. Cool on rack but leave oven set.

To make the filling, beat egg yolks until thick and light yellow. Add the condensed milk. While beating, add half of the lime and lemon juices. Add the other half after the first half is blended in. Add lime and lemon peel. Continue to mix until well blended. Pour into crust and bake for 10 to 12 minutes.

Just before serving, using a pastry bag, pipe *creme fraiche* on top. Serves 6 to 8.

Steve Lukather

"Luke" is probably best known as the founder of the band Toto, which he formed in 1978. Toto landed in the Top 10 with its self-titled LP and its major hit single "Hold the Line." Toto's biggest success came with *Toto IV* and the block-busters "Africa" and "Rosanna."

Luke is also one of the busiest session guitarists on the Los Angeles studio scene. His exceptional guitar playing can be heard on an astounding number of different artists' records—Eric Clapton, Cher, Earth, Wind, and Fire, Michael Jackson, Quincy Jones, Alice Cooper, Joe Cocker, Neil Diamond—the list goes on and on.

A prolific vocalist and composer as well, Luke continues to pursue a successful solo career as well as recording and touring the world with Toto.

Mr. and Mrs. Steve Lukather's Cherry Cheesecake 2002

It really does taste awesome and is very simple to make.

One 8-ounce package cream cheese, room temperature

One 14-ounce can sweetened condensed milk

⅓ cup lemon juice

1 teaspoon vanilla extract

2 cups graham crackers, crushed

½ cup butter, melted

⅓ cup fine sugar

One 21-ounce can of cherry pie filling

With a mixer, beat cream cheese and condensed milk in large bowl until smooth. Stir in lemon juice and vanilla. Set aside.

In a large bowl, mix crushed graham crackers, butter, and sugar until all crackers are moist. Press evenly into the bottom of a 9-inch pie plate. Chill for an hour or so. Pour cream cheese mixture evenly into chilled graham cracker crust. Chill at least 3 hours and top with cherry pie filling before serving.

Then, take out your bong, fire it up, and eat the whole damn thing! Hahahaha! Just kidding with this last line. Hahahahahahahaha!

Kathi Kamen Goldmark

Perhaps best known for founding and performing with the "writers-who-rock" all-author rock band, the Rock Bottom Remainders (Amy Tan, Stephen King, and Scott Turow are also members), Kathi Kamen Goldmark has made her mark on the literary stage by adding her novel *And My Shoes Keep Walking Back to You* to a penned collection that includes *The Great Rock & Roll Joke Book* and *Midlife Confidential*, a novel by and about the Rock Bottom Remainders.

As president and custodian of "Don't Quit Your Day Job" Records, Kathi has written and produced dozens of original songs, one of which was included in Stephen King's miniseries *The Stand*. Her label's 1998 release, *Stranger Than Fiction!* includes music performed by forty writers willing to sing their favorite songs for a good cause—the PEN Writers Special Fund. Two spoken-word releases feature Amy Tan and Maya Angelou.

Kathi performs regularly in San Francisco with her country-rock band Train Wreck, singing and playing rhythm guitar . . . and likes to think she is ready for anything.

Backstage with Kathi Kamen Goldmark . . .

What is your favorite food moment?

After a long and frustrating day, I gloomily opened the refrigerator knowing I would find nothing edible, let alone interesting. Imagine my delight when I discovered that my dear friend Lorraine Battle had let herself in and placed an "extra" chocolate swirl cheesecake next to my old jar of mustard and wilted celery. The generosity of my pal combined with the element of surprise elevated this dessert to "favorite food/food I would be" status in my book.

What is your favorite restaurant and favorite items on the menu?

West coast: You can't beat the Warm Goat Cheese Salad at Chez Panisse Café for a light lunch, or Fountain Court on Clement Street for a sensational Chinese dinner.

East coast: I have a weakness for Carmine's, my cousin's family-style Italian restaurant in New York City (there are two locations, one on the Upper West Side, the other in Times Square area). Go hungry, with a large group, for huge plates of pasta, calamari, roast chicken, and the best garlic spinach in the universe.

Food for thought . . .

My friend Roy Blount, Jr., has collected over 1,800 food songs on tape, and I have copies of most of them. They make great soundtracks for cooking. "That is Why You're Overweight" by Eddie Harris is a favorite.

What music would you recommend to accompany your recipe?

My own original food song makes an appearance in my first novel. In the story, "Dave and Michelle from Bruno's market" perform this in a talent show:

"Supermarket Fantasy."

m: I let you squeeze my melons down at the produce stand

d: I loved the way you held that ripe zucchini in your hand

m: You helped me grind my coffee

d: You sweetened up my tea

Both: We've never met but you're my supermarket fantasy

         I got the weekly special when you rolled your shopping cart

         Out of farm fresh vegetables and right into my heart

         I don't even know your name but I like what I see

         We've never met but you're my supermarket fantasy

d: Cakes and pies, big brown eyes, are pretty as can be

m: You're so hot, what you got meets all my baking needs

d: If I walk up and say hello, please answer with a smile

Both: And maybe someday, darling, we'll go walking down the aisle. . .

Sweet Lorraine's Chocolate Swirl Cheesecake

I dare you not to eat the whole thing in one sitting.

Crust

1¼ cups graham cracker crumbs

1 tablespoon sugar

¾ stick of butter, melted

Filling

1 pound (2 packages) cream cheese, softened

One 15-ounce container ricotta cheese

4 large eggs

1 cup sugar

2 teaspoons vanilla

1 tablespoon cocoa powder

1 teaspoon instant coffee

To make the crust, mix all three ingredients together and press into the bottom and sides of a 9- or 10-inch springform pan.

To make the filling, combine cream cheese, ricotta cheese, eggs, sugar and vanilla in a food processor until smooth. Remove 1 cup of the cream cheese mixture and mix in the cocoa powder and instant coffee.

Preheat oven to 325°F. Pour the cream cheese mixture from the food processor into the prepared springform pan. Drop spoonfuls of the chocolate cheesecake mixture into the mixture. Using a knife, make swirls in the cheesecake, making a pattern of swirls. Bake for 50 minutes. Cool and serve. Makes 8 to 10 servings.

Lauren Broersma-Cutler

Vocalist Lauren Broersma-Cutler lives her life in song. Being involved in various choirs, theatrical and musical groups over the years—most notably as the soulful, cohesive voice of the Tahoe-based Blue Nectar Band, which is showcased on their debut CD, *Tahoe Blue*—has given a musical foundation to her life.

In Lauren's view, "Our lives are a journey not unlike a musical score, complete with dissonance, harmonies, and startling crescendos. Music and food are not just entertainment, but the very expression of the struggles and triumphs of our lives."

Backstage with Lauren Broersma-Cutler . . .

If you were a food, what would you be?
Mango.

What is your favorite food?
Sushi, especially ahi, with lots of wasabi.

Have you written or recorded a song with food theme or title?
The band name, Blue Nectar, was chosen for Blue Agave Tequila. "Nectar Blue," the song, is about tequila as well.

Do you have any special "backstage food" requests?
Cereal and soy milk.

What is your favorite restaurant?

Hiro Sushi in Kings Beach, California, at Lake Tahoe (or *any* good sushi restaurant on the delivery day).

What song would you play while eating (or preparing) this?

Bebel Gilberto's "Tanto Tempo."

Chocolate Tofu Pudding

This is often mistaken for mousse, because it is so rich and creamy.

2 cups barley-sweetened chocolate chips

One 14-ounce package silken tofu

1 tablespoon oil or butter

2 teaspoons vanilla

Maple syrup to taste

Raspberries (optional)

Strawberries (optional)

Melt chips in double boiler. Blend tofu and other ingredients in a blender or food processor. Pour in melted chocolate and blend until smooth. Sweeten with maple syrup, according to taste, if desired.

Fancy food tip: Pour this mousse substitute into wine glasses and layer with raspberries and sliced strawberries. It is so thick it will create solid layers and a colorful display for dessert at any dinner party.

Refrigerate for 2 hours or more (if you can resist eating it that long!) before serving. Makes 4 servings.

Andy Hamilton

To get the full effect—heart's melting and melding, the dining room filled with romantic nuance, hopes running high—Andy *insists* that this luscious Italian dessert be served after a sensual meal of Pappardelle Genovese (see page 92 for the recipe and to go backstage with the chef).

Tiramisu

I've seen loads of recipes for this dish. . . . Trust me, this is the one. If I told you how I got this recipe I'd have a row with the wife, but be assured it came from an Italian. This is more than enough for two—next time just double the quantity!

½ pint or so of some strong, *real* espresso coffee (if you use instant coffee bad karma will eventually catch up with you)

Packet of sponge fingers (approximately 24 soft ladyfingers)

Marsala

2 large free-range eggs, separated

2 ounces icing sugar (about ⅓ to ½ cup powdered sugar)

250 grams (9 ounces or 1 heaping cup) mascarpone cheese

Spoon of drinking chocolate (unsweetened cocoa) for dusting

Make your espresso and add to this a generous slug of Marsala. Dip half the ladyfingers momentarily into this (but not long enough to make them soggy). Arrange the fingers on the bottom of a 7- to 10-inch oval serving dish.

Drizzle a bit more Marsala over the ladyfingers—in fact have a small glass yourself. Beat the egg yolks with the powdered sugar until creamy and blend in the cheese. Beat well.

Whisk the egg whites in a spotlessly clean bowl until soft peaks form, and fold these into the cheese mixture with a metal spoon, being careful not to lose their fluffiness.

Spoon half the mixture over the ladyfingers. Dip the rest of the ladyfingers in more of the coffee-Marsala mixture and make another layer (first ladyfingers then the rest of the creamy mixture). Dust well with drinking chocolate. That's it! Just cover with foil and leave in the fridge overnight. Makes 4 to 6 servings.

La Ferme
Tribute to Cream

Occasionally in life, the stars align, all timing is perfect, and all elements work together to nurture the creation of a masterpiece, however short-lived or time-less. Such is the story of Cream, the British power-trio that brought together the best of the best—*la crème de la crème*—to lay the precious foundation for the blues-rock and hard rock of the future. In 1966 three exceptional musicians joined talents and minds—blues master Eric Clapton on guitar, Ginger Baker on drums, and Jack Bruce on bass guitar.

In a mere three years, they sold more than 15 million records, immortalizing songs such as "Sunshine of Your Love," "I Feel Free," and the Willie Dixon classic "Spoonful," redefining the instrumentalist's role in rock along the way. And then, all too early, the phenomenon blazed out, and the band became a legend.

In tribute to Cream, this recipe from Chef Yves Gigot at La Ferme restaurant in Genoa, Nevada, (let us introduce you to this gem on page 50) is *la crème de la crème*, the best of the best . . . ever.

Crème de la Crème Brûlée

"La Crème Brûlée de la Ferme"—Chef Yves Gigot

7 fresh egg yolks

1 cup and a little more of regular fine sugar

3 cups fresh heavy whipping cream

1 cup fresh whole milk

2 fresh vanilla beans

Let's cook!

On a chopping board, open the vanilla beans with the point of a little knife from top to bottom, and carefully scrape that grainy, black paste—this is pure, fresh vanilla—and reserve.

In a stainless steel bowl, add together egg yolks, sugar, and vanilla and stir vigorously until the mixture becomes pale yellow. Now add milk and whipping cream and stir just to combine. Reserve in the fridge for 1 hour.

On a burner, bring about a quart of water to a boil. Preheat oven to 300°F. After the hour, remove your bowl from the fridge and skim the foam and bubbles off the top. Pour the liquid into little crème brûlée dishes and arrange the dishes in a big hotel pan. Pour hot, boiling water into the big hotel pan up to two-thirds [of the sides] of the dishes. Bake the [whole] thing with a lid for 1 hour.

Once cooked, remove the crème brûlée dishes from the water and cool them in the fridge for at least 2 hours. At the time of serving, sprinkle some regular, fine sugar on the top of the dish and just torch it down [with a culinary torch or under the broiler] until the sugar has given you his best color. Enjoy. Makes 6 servings.

Ben & Jerry's Ice Cream That Rocks!

We love Ben & Jerry's, and Ben & Jerry love music . . . or at least they like to make music we can *eat*. Sweet licks include Phish Food, a chocolate ice cream with gooey marshmallow and caramel swirls laced with fudge fish, and One Sweet Whirled—inspired by a Dave Matthews' song—a caramel-coffee-marshmallow, fudge-chip extravaganza (it's also a campaign to fight global warming). And of course, we all know about the beloved Jerry Garcia's Cherry Garcia.

In their "earth-shattering, finger-licking, lip-smacking cookbook," *Ben & Jerry's Homemade Ice Cream & Dessert Book*, the two supreme chefs of sweet cream and "wizards of chunk" even divulge the recipe for their #1 all-time bestseller, Cherry Garcia Ice Cream (it makes a "grateful" quart). So make a joyful noise, partake in a bit of social action, and indulge in some "euphoric ice cream eating" on Ben & Jerry.

Cherry Garcia Phish Food in One Sweet Whirled Rockin' Hot Fudge Sundae

Rockin' Hot Fudge Sauce
(recipe follows)

1 quart Ben & Jerry's Cherry Garcia
ice cream

1 quart Ben & Jerry's Phish Food
ice cream

1 quart Ben & Jerry's One Sweet
Whirled ice cream

Rockin' Hot Fudge Sauce

From Romancing the Stove

8 ounces unsweetened chocolate

1 pound butter

7 cups powdered sugar

3 cups heavy cream, unwhipped

Go to the store and get a pint each of these Ben & Jerry's cosmic rockin' flavors and prepare to indulge. In the meantime, cook up a batch of the Rockin' Hot Fudge Sauce to some tunes of the Jerry Garcia Band, Grateful Dead, Phish, and the Dave Matthews Band.

In a large, heavy saucepan over barely any heat (this takes patience, but don't blow it), melt chocolate and butter until smooth. Alternately whisk in powdered sugar and cream, and stir until shiny and smooth. Leave on low heat for 15 minutes, taking care not to boil. Stir occasionally. Makes approximately 1½ quarts of fudge (a lot).

To assemble the Cherry Garcia Phish Food in One Sweet Whirled Rockin' Hot Fudge Sundae, take a big bowl, dollop in a few scoops of each flavor and smother in Rockin' Hot Fudge Sauce. Continue rockin' out to your favorite tunes and consume *blissfully.*

Chapter 5

Jam Session

A Delicious Mix of Style and Tastes

Empañadas Fritas, Crema De Frijoles Negros, and Arroz Con Pollo—Madre's

Steak & Eggs—Joe Perry

Franklin's Outstanding Oatmeal—Tony Franklin

Welsh Cakes—Donna Lewis

Pennsylvania Funnel Cakes—Gordon Drysdale

Musician's Popcorn—Jamie Moses

Peanut Satay Sauce—Bob Weir

Sun-Dried Tomato Pesto—Michael Tobias

Hot Rod Hot Dogs & "Little Old Lady from Pasadena" Chocolate Fudge
Brownies—Tribute to Jan & Dean

Yummy Banana Bread—Will Hale

Peanut Butter on Toast Sandwiches with Corn Chips—Will Hale

Oatmeal Honey-Butter Biscuits—Steve Vai

Steve's Sticky Banana—Steve Vai

Madre's

Everyone has a favorite food that spells "H-O-M-E." Singer/actor/woman-of-the-world Jennifer Lopez shows us the way precisely to that hearty, soul-soothing meal: Madre's Restaurant. Nestled in the historic section of Pasadena, California, Madre's is a "family restaurant with a little bit of sexiness to it," created by Ms. Lopez to celebrate her cultural heritage and to lavish it on others.

In an "Old-Style Havana" ambiance, Chef Rolando Gonzales showcases a Latin cuisine—a perfect fusion of Puerto Rican and Cuban classics—inspired by the meals Jennifer's maternal grandmother served with love when she was growing up in the Bronx, New York. With his imaginative and authentic flair, Gonzales flawlessly recreates Ms. Lopez's touchstone favorites for *everyone* to enjoy.

If success is measured by the abundance of simple pleasures in life, like good food, a loving family, and a generous helping of upbeat, inspiring music and fun to glorify it all, then Jennifer Lopez has created her own hallmark of excellence. As a prodigious artist, she has gifted the whole world with her engaging style and playful, enfolding warmth in her music and on film. With her savvy offerings in fashion and fragrance, she has revealed a more sensuous and beautiful life to us, a place to relax and indulge.

Whatever our aspirations, J. Lo pulls out the recipe. In the "labor of love" and marvelous light she has established at Madre's, we see that the most important ingredients to personal joy certainly include a superb meal seasoned with the finest tradition and shared with excellent company.

Empañadas Fritas

This is a great party appetizer for family and friends that is as fun to prepare as it is to eat.

Dough

3¾ cups all-purpose flour

½ teaspoon salt

½ teaspoon sugar

8 tablespoons vegetable oil

2 large eggs

1 tablespoon dry white wine

8 tablespoons ice water

1½ quarts canola oil (for frying)

Filling

2 tablespoons extra-virgin olive oil

¾ pounds of each filling—shrimp or chicken (or asparagus and ricotta cheese—see note following)

1 cup onions, finely chopped

2 tablespoons garlic, minced

1 red bell pepper, finely chopped

1 green bell pepper, finely chopped

1 teaspoon ground cumin

¼ cup pimento-stuffed green olives, sliced

½ teaspoon salt

½ teaspoon freshly ground pepper

To make dough:

Place all dry ingredients in a bowl and mix well. Cut in vegetable oil and mix in eggs and the wine. Gradually add ice water by the tablespoon until soft dough forms, then gather dough and flatten into a disk. Wrap in plastic wrap and refrigerate for at least 30 minutes.

To make filling:

Heat olive oil in frying pan. Add your choice of filling (shrimp, chicken, or asparagus), onions, garlic, red and green peppers, and cumin and sauté. Cook until filling shows no signs of redness and vegetables are just tender. Add sliced pimento olives, salt, and pepper and set aside to cool. (Note: If using the ricotta cheese and asparagus filling, do not cook the ¾ pound of ricotta; just blend it in a blender and fold into asparagus sauté.)

Remove dough from refrigerator, cut in half and place on lightly floured surface. Roll out to about ¼-inch thickness, cut into 3-inch rounds with cutter, remove unused dough, then place rounds on tray. Place 1 tablespoon of filling ingredients onto the middle of the round dough. Moisten edges of dough with water; fold dough over filling and seal edges with tines of a fork. Set aside and continue until all rounds are filled. Roll out other half of dough and cut and fill.

Heat ½ quart of canola frying oil in large frying pan. When oil is hot (360°F), add a few empanadas to pan. Watching carefully, fry until golden in color, turning over with tongs. Drain on a paper towel. Add more oil and continue to fry in small batches until done. Makes 16 servings of 3 empanadas per person.

Crema De Frijoles Negros

This is a traditional Cuban classic: cream of black beans garnished with mashed potatoes.

3 quarts water

2 tablespoons salt

1 pound black beans

1 red bell pepper, julienne

1 bay leaf

1 garlic clove, finely chopped

1 large onion, finely chopped

¼ cup olive oil

2 green bell peppers, diced

1 teaspoon dried oregano

½ teaspoon freshly ground black pepper

Salt to season

2 tablespoons red vinegar

1 teaspoon sugar

Wash and rinse the black beans. In a large cooking pot on the stove, bring the water and salt to a boil; add the black beans. When the beans start to get soft, add the red bell pepper, bay leaf, half of the chopped garlic, and half of the chopped onions.

When the beans are soft, quickly sauté the rest of the chopped onions, garlic, green bell peppers, and oregano in olive oil for 2 minutes [in a large frying pan] until lightly brown. Add a little bit of black beans [from the pot] to incorporate the flavors.

Reincorporate the sautéed mixture to the pot of beans. Season with salt and pepper to taste, and cook on high heat until the beans have thickened. Turn off heat, add red vinegar and sugar, and you are ready to serve. Garnish with mashed potatoes. Makes ten 12-ounce servings.

Arroz Con Pollo

This is a wonderful chicken entrée served with Valencia yellow rice.

4 pounds whole chicken quarters

Marinade

2 garlic cloves, finely chopped

White wine (enough to cover the chicken)

Sauté medley

4 garlic cloves, finely chopped

1 large white onion, chopped

2 green bell peppers, diced

4 tablespoons of extra-virgin olive oil

2 bay leaves

½ cup beer (your choice)

½ cup white wine

3 tablespoons chicken stock or bouillon

½ teaspoon saffron or bijol

Rice

1 pound Valencia rice

2 cups water

1 cup sweet peas

4 ounces green pimento-stuffed Spanish olives, sliced

½ teaspoon salt

½ teaspoon freshly ground black pepper

3 red bell peppers, roasted, for garnish

Marinate the chicken for 2 hours in a mixture of chopped garlic and white wine.

In a large pan, sauté the garlic, onions, green bell peppers, and bay leaves in olive oil for 3 minutes until brown. Add the marinated chicken and sear it on both sides. Add your favorite beer, white wine, bouillon, and saffron; cook for 10 minutes or until the chicken is fully cooked.

Combine the Valencia rice with water and cook slowly over a low temperature for 15 minutes. Then add the sweet peas and pimento-stuffed olives, and season with salt and pepper. Turn of the heat and let the rice rest for 5 minutes covered.

When you are ready to serve, place the chicken and rice on a plate and decorate with the roasted red bell peppers. Makes four 16-ounce servings.

Joe Perry

Joe Perry, the laid-back guitar ace for the Boston-based arena-rock super-act Aerosmith, who picked up and played his first guitar (homemade by his uncle) at age six, hooked up with bandmates Steven Tyler and Tom Hamilton in the summer of 1970, and the rest is rock history. With mega-hits such as prototype power-ballad "Dream On" and riff-heavy tunes like "Sweet Emotion" and "Walk This Way," they set the style and sound for hard rock for the next two decades . . . and they're still going strong.

Guitar in one hand and a bottle of his Rock Your World Boneyard Brew Hot Sauce in the other, Joe, along with Aerosmith frontman and singer Steven Tyler, is also proud part-owner of Mount Blue, a rockin' restaurant in the Boston 'burb of Norwell that serves an American café-style menu with an ethnic twist and showcases some of the best-quality musical entertainment around.

Backstage with Joe Perry . . .

If you were a food, what would you be?

Whatever my wife put down as her favorite food.

What is your favorite food?

Meat . . . BBQ.

Favorite restaurants and favorite items on the menu . . .

Mount Blue in Boston (home)—Osso Bucco. Il Cortina in NYC—Anything. L.C.'s in K.C.—Ribs.

Do you have any special "backstage food" requirements?

Everything must be fresh.

Food for thought . . .

If you're ever in Boston, check out Mount Blue.

What music would you recommend playing to accompany your recipe?

"Mannish Boy" by Muddy Waters.

Steak & Eggs

Filet mignon leftovers

Olive oil

3 eggs, separated into 2 egg yolks
and 3 egg whites

5 drops water

Salt and pepper to taste

2 pieces of whole grain toast

Rock Your World Boneyard Brew
Hot Sauce

Take leftover filet mignon from the night before and slice ½-inch thick. Grill in frying pan with olive oil for about a minute.

Add eggs (2 yolks, 3 whites) and turn heat down. When the [egg] whites turn almost white, add a little salt and fresh pepper and 5 drops of water and cover. Just when yolks turn slightly milky, take off the stove (you want the yolk runny and the white loose, but not runny).

Heat your plate with hot water, dry off, and transfer the steak and eggs to the plate. Two toasted slices of a good, wholegrain bread round out the meal. All it needs now is a dab of Rock Your World Hot Sauce! (For information on how to secure your hot sauce stash and really rock your Steak & Eggs, see All Access on page 269.) Serves 1 hungry guitarist.

Tony Franklin

Born into a musical family, six-year-old Tony began performing on a variety of instruments with his parents' band, the Jean Franklin Sound, whose specialty was "music for all occasions." At age eleven, his parents gave him a bass guitar and he knew it was the instrument for him. After practicing for only three days, he was ready to tour as a bass player.

Before embarking on a solo career in 1991, Tony worked his fretless magic on bands like the Firm, Blue Murder, and Whitesnake, playing with some of the biggest names in rock, including Paul Rodgers, Jimmy Page, David Coverdale, and David Gilmour.

A consummate musician and creative force, Tony plays, sings, and writes, and has the technical savvy to get it all recorded and Pro-tooled to completion. Yet in his exciting live performances, he plays with carefree abandon . . . sometimes barefoot!

Backstage with Tony Franklin . . .

What is your favorite food?

When I was a child, I used to have a saying: "Of all the things I like to do, the best of all is eating!" So I would say that my favorite food is whatever's on my plate in front of me! More specifically, Japanese food is probably my favorite, followed closely by Mexican food.

If you were a food, what would you be?

That's easy—Superfood (Hmm . . . does this count as a food?). Superfood is a nutritional green drink that contains spirulina, wheat grass, barley grass, algae—and you guessed it—seaweed!

Favorite restaurants and favorite items on the menu . . .

Mako Sushi in Studio City, California . . . the Chili Dofu, a huge soup-broth dish with cod, vegetables, tofu, and noodles; also their Natto Sushi, Tempura Vegetables, Kimpira, Hijiki, Green Tea, and Tempura Ice Cream! It's *all* good!

Leonor's Vegetarian Mexican Restaurant in Studio City, California . . . the Buffalo Bill Burrito with added cilantro. I've been going to this place for ten years, and I think this is the only dish I've had, except for their Vegetarian Pizza—Mmmmm!

Real Food Daily in Santa Monica, California . . . T.V. Dinner (veggie "meatloaf" with mashed potatoes, gravy, vegetables) or "Real Food Meal," a macrobiotic feast! Okay, I'm getting hungry now!

Have you written/recorded a song with a food theme or title?

When I was about sixteen years old, I wrote and recorded a punky little tune called "The Seaweed Song." (What! You mean you never heard it?!) One of the lines in the song was a spoken joke: "Why was the beach wet? . . . Because the sea weed!"

Do you have any special "backstage food" requirements on tour?

I request vegetarian food and then I leave it up to the catering (I figure that any catering company that's booked for a big tour knows what they're doing!) and enjoy the surprises. As far as nibbles go, I like some raw vegetables (organic, if possible), mixed, unsalted nuts, and *lots* of water!

What song would you recommend playing while preparing this signature recipe?

Well, personally I find it hard to play bass and cook at the same time, but as for playing a CD, I would recommend anything by Stevie Wonder. Hmmm . . . thinking about it though, it's not easy for me to resist dancing when Stevie's playing! Oh the challenges we musicians have!

Franklin's Outstanding Oatmeal

"FOO"

I think because I'm English, I was instilled with the importance of eating a good breakfast in the morning. The wisdom behind this probably came from the days when the menfolk would eat a hearty breakfast before going out for a hard day's work in the fields or down a mine shaft. My work routine is different from theirs, but even so, when I'm "fueled up" in the morning, I feel like I'm ready to take on the world! This dish is quick and easy to prepare.

3 cups water

¼ cup raisins

Sea salt (optional)

1½ cups whole, rolled oats

¼ cup pecans, chopped

Fresh banana, sliced

Dried cranberries or dried cherries (optional)

Soy or regular milk

Ground cinnamon to taste

Sweetener of choice (Stevia is my favorite)

Dash of salt (optional)

Bring the water, with raisins added, to a slow boil in a stainless steel or heavy glass saucepan. Add a pinch of sea salt, if desired. As the water starts to boil, stir in the whole, rolled oats. Turn down heat to low and simmer, stirring occasionally (make sure it doesn't burn!).

Cook for 6 to 8 minutes, until the texture is right (most of the water is absorbed and the oatmeal is soft but not mushy). Turn off the heat and let the oatmeal sit for a few minutes.

Give the oatmeal one more stir and then serve! Put the oatmeal into individual bowls (be sure you have a big enough bowl) and sprinkle some pecans, banana slices, and dried cranberries or cherries on top, if desired. Stir in some soy or regular milk, sprinkle on some cinnamon and sweetener to taste, and add a dash of salt, if desired. Find some hungry musicians (usually very easy!) and *enjoy!* Serves 3 to 4.

Rehearsal Notes

♪ Tony adds, "The quantities for everything, except the oatmeal and water, are really down to individual taste, and hunger! This recipe serves 3 to 4 people, but to increase the serving size, simply increase the amount of water and oats, while maintaining the ratio of 2 to 1 (water to oats)."

♪ And to make your breakfast complete, Tony recommends "a Superfood shake during or before your FOO in the morning. This nutritional powerhouse will give a kickstart to your day anytime (and it tastes great!). It is not available in the stores, but for more information call (800) HERB-DOC (no I'm not a rep!)."

Donna Lewis

Born and raised in the Welsh city of Cardiff and trained in flute and piano at the Welsh College of Music and Drama, Donna Lewis went on to perform with local bands, and by 1990 was working solo in piano bars across Britain and Europe. After some of her demo tapes made their way to the chairman of Atlantic Records, Donna found herself flying to New York to meet with Doug Morris, who offered her a contract on the spot.

Donna's debut album *Now in a Minute* contained the up-tempo hit song "I Love You Always Forever," which took the album platinum. *Blue Planet* produced two more hit singles, followed by *Be Still* in 2002, proving that this major talent is here to stay! Donna's voice can also be heard on the soundtrack for *Anastasia*.

Backstage with Donna . . .

What is your favorite food?
Sushi.

If you were a food, what would you be?
Pineapple.

What song would you recommend playing while preparing this?
"It's Not Unusual" by Tom Jones.

Welsh Cakes

Hope everyone loves the Welsh cakes!!

225 grams (approximately 1⅓ cups) flour

½ teaspoon baking powder

Pinch of mixed spice or nutmeg

125 grams (2 tablespoons) butter

75 grams (approximately ½ cup) sugar

75 grams (approximately ⅔ cup) currants

1 large egg, beaten

A little milk

Sugar for topping

Rub [cut] the butter into the spiced flour [with baking powder blended in]. Add the sugar and currants, and bind with beaten egg and a little milk (if needed) to a stiffish paste.

Preheat oven to 350°F. Roll dough out on a floured board to about ¼ inch thick. Cut into 2½-inch rounds [with a pastry or cookie cutter] and bake on a hot bakestone or nonstick pan for 3 to 5 minutes each side until golden brown. Sprinkle with sugar before serving. Makes approximately 15 "scone-like" cakes.

Gordon Drysdale

When Gordon's not jamming with the Back Burner Blues Band (see page 19), you'll find him in full pizza-god regalia flipping the finest "Old World Style meets New World Taste" pies for Pizza Antica, the coolest pizza joint in San Jose, California. Formerly the owner-chef for the well-loved but now legendary San Francisco restaurant Gordon's House of Fine Eats—*the* place where food, art, and music met—Gordon still promises that at Pizza Antica, "We are more comfortable and more delicious than ever." Gordon rocks.

Pennsylvania Funnel Cakes

This is a recipe for my favorite of our way cool Doughnut Plate [that everyone loved] at Gordon's House of Fine Eats.

2 quarts canola oil	1½ teaspoons baking powder
2 cups milk	1 teaspoon vanilla extract
2 large egg yolks	Scrapings from 1 vanilla bean
3¼ cups all-purpose flour	½ teaspoon salt
½ cup sugar	Powdered sugar
2 teaspoons baking soda	

Heat the canola oil to 375°F in a large heavy pot. While oil is heating, beat the milk and egg yolks together in a medium bowl. Add the rest of the ingredients and stir until smooth.

Transfer the batter to a pastry bag with a #3 tip and pipe directly into the hot oil (it will take about 1 minute to cook all the way through). Remove from oil and drain on paper towels. Dust heavily with powdered sugar and serve! Makes 8 servings.

Jamie Moses

One of Great Britain's top session guitarists, Jamie has been a member of such bands as the Pretenders, Broken English, and the Brian May Band. Most recently he has toured with Bob Geldof, Paul Young, and Los Pacaminos, as well as performing with Queen and the S.A.S. Band and doing his own solo shows. He also worked with guitar legend Pete Townsend on the West End production of *Tommy*, and toured with the *Elvis* musical earlier in his career.

Touring is not an easy gig, but Jamie brings a sense of fun to every project, and his presence in a band guarantees that a good time will be had by all!

Backstage with Jamie Moses . . .

What is your favorite food?

Chili con carne.

If you were a food, what would you be?

Spud-U-Like!

Do you have a favorite restaurant and a favorite item on the menu?

The Chicken in Black Bean Sauce at Ghurkha Kitchen in Oxted, Surrey, England.

Do you have any special "backstage food" requests?

Fried chicken.

Food for thought . . .

The best songs are like popcorn; they should take no longer than 3 minutes, be digestible by anyone, and leave you wanting more.

Can you suggest music to accompany this recipe?

Theme from *Superman*.

Musician's Popcorn

1. Buy microwave popcorn (any make).

2. Remove plastic wrapper.

3. Place in microwave [and pop] per manufacturer's instructions.

4. Listen for "ding" sound.

5. Put beer down.

6. Remove from oven and decant into bowl that no one has been sick in.

7. Pick up beer with right hand.

8. Walk toward couch.

9. Return to kitchen, pick up popcorn with left hand while still holding beer with right hand.

10. Walk toward couch again.

11. Place popcorn on coffee table and lie on couch.

12. Once settled (make sure TV remote is accessible from this position), place bowl on chest.

13. If guests ask to share your popcorn, tell them to piss off and make their own (unless they're prepared to get you another beer).

14. Fall asleep.

Bob Weir

Our first responsibility is to amuse ourselves; if we can't do that, then we can't entertain anyone.

—*Bob Weir*

In an interview years back, when asked how success had changed him (and the Grateful Dead at that time), rhythm guitarist and troubadour Bob Weir philosophized, "I was noticing the other night, for instance, when I'm going through pistachios, opening pistachios . . . the hard-to-open ones? I don't bother with them any more—who's got time?"

Fortunately for fans, this Grateful Gourmet who "has a passion for food second only to music," found a nick of time a while back between tours, time on stage with band Ratdog, and enjoying life to concoct a line of hot-licks hot sauces and share a favorite recipe for this zesty satay sauce (see page 277 of All Access for ordering information). Weir, a strict vegetarian who eats "nothing with a head," is playing in the band once again with the Dead, a resurrected musical feast being shared by all surviving members of the Grateful Dead.

Peanut Satay Sauce

From Food Men Love

6 tablespoons Weir's Otherworld
Wok Sauce or Snake Oil Stir Fry

6 tablespoons chunky peanut butter

6 tablespoons lite coconut milk

1 teaspoon maple syrup

Combine all ingredients in a bowl. Serve Weir's Peanut Satay Sauce as a dipping sauce with skewers of headless grilled vegetables (portobello mushrooms, eggplant, baby bok choy, zucchini) or brush on veggies or some type of meat substitute like firm tofu or Boca Burgers and grill. Makes approximately 1 cup of satay sauce.

Rehearsal Notes

♪ In all respect to Mr. Weir, this satay sauce is also delicious on grilled foods that once had heads, like chicken and assorted seafood.

Michael Tobias

Michael Tobias began building guitars and basses in 1974, selling his first company to Gibson and now hand-crafting about ten instruments a month at his Michael Tobias Design studio in upstate New York. Using different combinations of woods (preferably from managed forests), he creates electric and acoustic instruments with ergonomic designs and a variety of tonal qualities that add just the right flavor to such varied musical dishes as Riverdance and Jimmy Buffett, Santana and Koko Taylor, Suicidal Tendencies and the Statler Brothers.

When cooking up a batch of MTD basses, Michael prowls the lumberyard, turning over ash and maple, squinting at alder and tulipwood like some portly, white-bearded chef combing the fishmarket for the freshest clams and cuttlefish for his cioppino.

Backstage with Michael Tobias . . .

What is your favorite food?
Oriental of all kinds.

If you were a food, what would you be?
Espresso!

Favorite restaurant . . . Favorite items on the menu?
Victor's Café Cuban Restaurant in Manhattan . . . the Vacca Frita or Ropa Vieja.

What song would you suggest playing while eating (or preparing) your recipe?
The Allman Brothers' "Don't Want You No More" or Jeff Beck's "Freeway Jam."

Sun-Dried Tomato Pesto

The sun-dried tomato pesto is wonderful on fresh bread or spread on portobello mushrooms that are broiled and topped with grated Romano.

2 cups sun-dried tomatoes

Water (for soaking tomatoes)

4 large cloves of garlic, peeled

¼ to ½ cup Asiago or Romano cheese

¼ cup pignolias (pine nuts)

¼ cup almonds

⅛ teaspoon salt

2 cups extra-virgin olive oil, divided

Soak tomatoes in water or cover them in water and heat in microwave for about 2 minutes. Drain and put them in a food processor with the chopping blade. Add some of the olive oil and turn on the machine. While the machine is running, add more oil as the tomatoes begin turning into paste. Add garlic, then the cheese and salt, and begin to add the nuts a bit at a time, alternating with the remaining oil. (You may need to add additional oil depending on the consistency of the paste. I usually like it moist, so I sometimes add an additional ½ to 1 cup oil.)

Rehearsal Notes

♪ Michael adds, "You can also make a great 'almost regular' pesto by using 2 cups fresh young basil leaves in place of the tomatoes—no stems—and adding about 1 cup of parboiled broccoli. In a traditional pesto there would only be some basil and a bit of milk—a tablespoon or so with the cheese, nuts, etc.—and the broccoli takes away some of the bitterness."

Jan & Dean

What began as a couple of guys rehearsing for a school talent show in Jan Berry's parents' garage, circa 1958, became one of the most successful vocal groups ever to capture the sound of California surf music. With their musical roots in doo wop, Jan & Dean (Torrence), along with another local band, the Beach Boys, capitalized on the "surf song" and "hot rod" beach beat genres that were exploding in the So-Cal sun-soaked early '60s. Hit upon hit, including "Surf City," "Drag City," and "The Little Old Lady from Pasadena" (who was actually from Oxnard) lit up the airwaves.

One song, "Dead Man's Curve," proved to be eerily and tragically prophetic: in 1966, at the age of twenty-five, at the top of his game, Jan Berry crashed his new Stingray on a curvy side street, forever changing these two stars' course. Twelve years after Jan's accident, Jan & Dean made a remarkable comeback and have since put in another twenty years, and still singing together along with Dean's band, the Surf City Allstars. Jan & Dean even played in the People's Republic of China, where Dean was the first person ever to skateboard on the Great Wall of China.

Backstage with Jan & Dean . . .

Jan:

If you were a food, what would you be?

A fudge brownie.

What is your favorite food?

Caesar salad, chocolate fudge brownies, Famous Amos cookies.

Dean:

If you were a food, what would you be?

A hot dog.

Jan & Dean:

Have you ever recorded a song with food in the theme or title?

"Popsicle."

Hot Rod Hot Dogs

For Dean

From Food Men Love, Courtesy of Charlie Girsch

2 of your favorite off-the-shelf hot dogs

2 of your favorite white bread hot dog buns

Ketchup, mustard, relish, onions, tomatoes, celery salt, ground black pepper, and a hot pepper or two if you can stand the heat

Simmer the hot dogs in water in a large saucepan (that can accommodate a colander). When the color is cooked out, nestle a colander in the saucepan above the water to catch the rising steam. (Leave the hot dogs in the water to keep them warm.) Place the separated buns face down in the colander and turn off the heat. Cover with a lid and let the steam caress the buns for a minute or two (you might lose a bun or two to the super sogs while perfecting your bun-warming technique, but persist).

Deposit each hot dog carefully in a warmed bun and slather on the condiments. Before you take that first bite, shake celery salt all over it, maybe a sprinkle of ground pepper, and enjoy! Surf's up! Makes 2 rockin' dogs.

"Little Old Lady from Pasadena" Chocolate Fudge Brownies

For Jan
From Romancing the Stove

1 pound (2 cups) butter

8 ounces unsweetened solid chocolate

4 cups sugar

8 eggs

2 teaspoons pure vanilla extract

¾ teaspoon salt

2¼ cups unbleached white flour

2 cups chocolate chips (semisweet or milk chocolate, your choice)

1 (or more) cups chopped walnuts (optional)

Slowly melt the butter and chocolate together on low, low, low heat in a very large, heavy saucepan. While they are melting, grease and flour a large sheet or jelly-roll pan or two 9 x 13 x 2-inch pans (a commercial 12 x 17-inch "half-flat" is the ideal size).

Stir the melted chocolate and butter together, add the sugar, and mix well with a wooden spoon. Allow this chocolate syrup to remain on the stove for about 5 minutes so the sugar melts completely. (If you want to take a short cut, you can skip this stovetop process altogether and microwave the butter and chocolate—and then the sugar—on low in a large bowl until all is melted and smooth.)

Preheat the oven to 325°F. In a separate, large bowl (not any smaller than 8 quarts), beat the eggs, vanilla, and salt together by hand with a wooden spoon (do not use an electric mixture). While stirring, add the chocolate syrup to the egg mixture; stir until it becomes shiny.

Gently stir in flour until smooth, then add the chocolate chips. Pour into pan or pans. At this point, feel free to toss a few handfuls of chopped walnuts on top of the batter if you like nuts on your brownies.

Bake for 25 to 28 minutes, no more. You will either have to trust this recipe or rely on your instinct to tell if they are done. Cool before cutting while jamming to some vintage Jan & Dean. Makes 4 dozen 2-inch square Chocolate Fudge Brownies.

Will Hale

With his voice, guitar, drums, percussion instruments, harmonica, and mandolin all tuned in and up, Will Hale launched his full-time music career in 1989. In his appreciation for the enthusiasm, receptivity, and vivid imagination of children, this rollicking and inspired Pied Piper has focused his musical gift primarily on children and families, providing a unique mix of musical styles with a dynamic range of emotion and live performances and recordings that are filled with plenty of surprises and good-time fun.

His first recording, *I Love Everything*, features an enthusiastic diversity of musical styles, from original feel-good tunes to a beautiful cover of the Grateful Dead lullaby "Brokedown Palace." The fun interactive music on his *Perfect World* CD continues with themes of cooperation, positive self-esteem, and tunes to bring out the kid in everyone. Proving you're never too old to feel young, Will has also created the Tadpole Parade Fun Club, an online adventure for families and kids . . . of all ages.

Backstage with Will Hale . . .

What is your favorite food?

Fresh walleye.

If you were a food, what would you be?

A whole cashew.

Favorite restaurant and favorite item on the menu?

Ichiban in Minneapolis—the Teppanyaki-style Scallops and Veggies.

Do you have any special "backstage food" requests?

On national tours I like to have plenty of Tazo Brambleberry juiced tea around as well as Cliff Bars or similar nutritious, protein energy bars.

Have you written or recorded songs with a food theme or title?

"The Garden Song" is about growing food. "Big Feelings" mentions feeling hungry.

Can you suggest music to accompany this recipe?

"I Love Everything" . . . and I would also highly recommend making up your own verses!

Yummy Banana Bread

When I was growing up, I wouldn't eat bananas very often because I knew if I let them get black and ripe my mom would make banana bread. During the recording of Perfect World my mom made several loaves of homemade banana bread, which were enthusiastically devoured by everyone at the studio. This is a longtime favorite Hale family recipe (from Judith Hale, . . . who received it from her coworker Cleo at her first job at Holm & Olson in 1957).

1 cup sugar	3 ripe bananas, mashed
¼ cup shortening	1¾ cups flour
2 eggs	1 teaspoon baking soda
3 tablespoons sour milk (add ½ teaspoon of vinegar to milk to make it sour)	Dash of salt

Cream the sugar, shortening, eggs, and sour milk in a mixing bowl. Add bananas and mix. Then add the flour, baking soda, and salt and stir together.

Preheat oven to 350°F. Lightly grease a (preferably) 12 x 4 x 2½ -inch cake pan. Pour in the mixture and bake at for approximately 45 minutes. (The top will get browned and you can test to see if it's finished baking by putting a knife or toothpick in the center; if it pulls out clean, it's finished!) Let cool for 5 to 10 minutes before removing from the pan and slicing. Enjoy! Makes one yummy loaf.

Peanut Butter on Toast Sandwiches with Corn Chips

This is one of my favorite, super-simple delicacies.

New England brown bread (see
note following)

Bearitos salted yellow corn chips

All-natural peanut butter, no
added sugar (salt is okay)

For the optimal sandwich I would recommend:

Toasting two slices of New England brown bread. Generously slather both
pieces with peanut butter. Add Bearitos corn chips to one side. Smoosh both
[slices of bread] together and enjoy a crunchy, tasty sandwich!

Rehearsal Notes

𝄞 New England brown bread is a very sensible, hearty bread made with
leftover bread pieces, rye meal, corn meal, molasses, and graham flour.
It is produced and sold commercially, and there are also good recipes to
be found in cookbooks and on the Internet. Just go to *www.google.com*
and type in "New England brown bread." Then follow the brown bread
brick road!

Steve Vai

Steve Vai's astounding technical mastery earned him the nickname "Seven String Sorcerer" from David Coverdale of Whitesnake. When Steve straps on his guitar, magnificent complementary layers of sound emerge, weaving intricate sonic tapestries.

Steve first gained notice as a young hotshot guitar slinger with Frank Zappa, a man famed for his intolerance for the musical imposter. Steve was also a member of the David Lee Roth Band and Whitesnake before going solo.

A true virtuoso, this Grammy-nominated guitarist is comfortable in any style, from heavy metal to fusion to fronting a full classical orchestra. Along with former teacher Joe Satriani, Steve helped define rock guitar history throughout the '80s.

Backstage with Steve . . .

When we were living in Hollywood our neighbors had honey bees in the wall of their home. As a result our garden looked great because they are the #1 pollinators. (About one-third of the human diet is derived from insect-pollinated plants and honey bees are responsible for 80 percent of this pollination.)

We later moved to a two-acre home in Encino that had been abandoned for ten years by a kooky millionaire. The grounds were dilapidated. Pia [my wife] wanted to plant gardens, and I wanted to put in some fruit trees, so I went online and did a little research and found out how to keep and take care of honey bees. It's really very easy and an interesting and eclectic hobby, so I got a swarm and eventually that turned into five colonies (hives).

Well, [our] bees make serious honey. We do a party-like honey harvest once a year and usually pull close to 1,000 liquid pounds of honey. What do [we] do with it all besides send it out as X-mas gifts?

Naturally made from wildflowers, honey is all-natural with no additives or preservatives and will bring new enlightenment to your muffin! Honey has been known to keep for 2,000 years and still be edible. (If you don't believe me, save a bottle for 2,000 years, or even just a few hundred years, and try it on some toast. I bet you'll be pleased!) All honey will eventually crystallize, but can be returned to its natural consistency with a little heating.

Following are some uses for honey that you may not have thought of:

1. Obviously it's nice in tea, but I use it in coffee too. It has more nutrients and is much easier to digest than sugar.

2. Take some roasted or raw almonds with equal part honey and put it in the blender. It makes these unbelievably wonderful, hand-shape-able bars of gold.

3. Drizzle it on ice cream or cereal.

4. When you feel a sore throat coming on, take a spoonful and let it sit in your throat. It has tremendous therapeutic value. Many M.D.s used to carry a bottle of honey around with them when they made house calls (remember those days?) for many of the ailments their patients had.

5. Use it on your oatmeal instead of sugar.

6. I always keep a big jar of honey in the studio because nothing soothes a singer's throat better [than honey].

There has been much research done on the therapeutic value of honey—from healing cuts to alleviating allergies—but the best use of honey that we have found is in the bedroom when you have sex. You put it on the outside door handle so the kids can't get in.

I'm not much of a cook, but following is my sticky addition to your book; here [are two] recipes we like.

Oatmeal Honey-Butter Biscuits

Biscuits

2¼ cups flour

½ cup plus 2 tablespoons old-fashioned rolled oats (not quick-cooking), divided

2 teaspoons baking soda

1 teaspoon salt

⅔ cup solid vegetable shortening

¾ cup buttermilk

⅓ cup honey

Honey-Butter Topping

2 tablespoons honey

2 tablespoons butter, melted

2 tablespoons old-fashioned rolled oats (not quick-cooking)

Preheat oven to 400°F. Grease and flour a large baking sheet (or line it with baking parchment) and set aside.

To make the biscuits:

Combine flour, oats, baking soda, and salt in large bowl. Stir until well combined. Add the shortening to flour mixture and cut in with a pastry cutter or two forks, until the mixture is crumbly. Add buttermilk and honey to the flour mixture; stir with a fork just until the liquids are absorbed and a soft dough forms.

Transfer dough to a well-floured work surface, and using well-floured hands, pat into a ⅓-inch thick circle. Dust the top of the dough with flour. Using a 2½-inch biscuit cutter or drinking glass, cut out the biscuits.

Place biscuits 2 inches apart on the prepared baking sheet. Recombine dough trimmings and reflour work surface. Pat out trimmings to ⅓-inch thickness and repeat entire process to make as many additional biscuits as possible.

To make the honey-butter topping:

Place honey in a small bowl with melted butter. Stir until well mixed. Brush the tops of the biscuits lightly with the honey-butter mixture and sprinkle them with oats. Bake 15 minutes or until lightly browned. Transfer to wire rack to cool 10 minutes. Makes 15 to 18 biscuits.

Steve's Sticky Banana

8 wooden craft sticks

1⅓ cups topping (such as ground, toasted almonds, toasted coconut, candy sprinkles, or graham cracker crumbs)

4 "just-ripe" bananas, peeled

½ cup honey

Spread toppings of your choice on a plate or plates. Cut bananas in half crosswise. Insert a craft stick into each cut end. To assemble, hold 1 banana over plate or waxed paper to catch drips. Spoon about 1 tablespoon of honey over [each] banana, rotating and smoothing honey with back of spoon to coat all sides (or squeeze honey from a plastic honey bear container and smooth out with spoon).

Roll banana in topping of choice until coated on all sides, pressing with fingertips to help topping adhere. Place pops on waxed paper-lined cookie sheet. Repeat with remaining bananas, honey, and toppings. Serve at once. Makes 8 servings.

After-Show Party

Acknowledgments

First and foremost, we are most grateful to our "players"—the musicians, artists, families, and friends who shared their recipes, time, and "food for thought." Thank you so much for making this project a success.

We also raise a full glass in thanks to all of the messengers, managers, assistants, and scribes who were instrumental in helping us produce this culinary concert:

Sheri Fobare, Terry McBride, Caren Berger, Sara Bricusse, John Brother, Mick Cater, Sally Frost, Kim Godreau, Tim Gooch, Betty J. Handy, Mashariki Williamson, Laura Kaufman, Emily Lodge, Michael McIntyre, Linda Peterson, Donatella Piccinetti, Mike Alexander, Joe Bordeau, Nicholas Brown, Shawn Comstock, Tricia Wintch, Tony Franklin, Derek Hilland, Michael and Luanne Hirsh, Richard Poudrier, Pam Simpkins, Bjorn Thorsrud, Chris Whitemeyer, Kim Thomas, Dennis McNally, Ambrosia Healy, Nina Avramides, Alfred S. Regnery and Gwen Nappi at Regnery Publishing, Inc., Anita at Fitzgerald Hartley Company, an enormous "thank you" to Kyle Verwers, who went way beyond the call of duty, and of course, Jimmy Eyers, John Bionelli, and Tom Higgins at the Aerosmith Office. Lisa Walker, thank you for helping keep all "your guys" up on the deadlines—we so appreciate you for that!

Also, a special toast to Sharon Callaly, Sheila Roche, Ailish Cantwell at the Clarence, Wassim Boustani at Madre's, Cathy Hendrix, Beth Bachtold, Abbey Tyson, Ben Fong-Torres, Jeff and Paula Pensiero, Debra Andrade, Emily DeHuff, Chuck Chejfec, Anamaria Cashman, and Claire Thomas at Freedom from Hunger—you all rock!

To "the wives" who helped make many of these recipes and questionnaires *actually* materialize:

Stacy Aldrich, Karen Aldridge, Debbie Beach, Sadhna Bissonette, Caroline Bossi, Elvira Drury, Heidi Franklin, Rachel Hamilton, Lory Keller-Butcher, Shawn Ligertwood, Jacqueline Love, Denise Martin, Leah Mendoza, Dabar "Rivera," Joanne Stassi, Margot Steinberg-Harrison, Debbie Tuggle, Pia Vai, Amy Goff, and Saskia Van Roosmalen. Thank you all.

Many delicious thanks to our intrepid recipe "tester and taster" team: Laura Velasco, Joi Scheele, Stacy Aldrich, Debbie Hansen, Jennifer Lee, Suzanne Tarrantino, Suzanne Shapiro, Laurel Champlin, Alex and Ben Narasin, Shahri Masters, Suzan Kennedy, Cathy Norris, and everyone who lent their taste buds and kitchens.

Susie Zweigle, Debbie and Richard Poudrier, Julie Freeman, Christie Lee, Kim Grow, Bonnie Flynn, and Yvette Beebe, you are the best—truly, Y. B. Uglee when it's fun to be beautiful!

To our great publishing crew at Red Wheel/Weiser and Conari Press, we are so grateful for your enthusiasm and all of your hard work and help—Let's rock and enjoy the show!

Leslie Berriman, you "frisky redhead," you saw the dream and set the stage for it to come alive; and to the rockin' goddess Brenda Knight, for your savvy marketing magic—the champagne is on us! Thank you.

Cindy's VIPs

I would very much like to thank those people I am so fortunate to have in my life who truly made this a joy-filled experience and who helped out in a variety of ways:

Laura Velasco you are amazing! Thank you so much for all of your help, allowing me to be at my computer knowing dinner would be put on the table and my boys would be taken care of. You are an angel.

Ken Ciancimino, thank you for spreading the word—a couple of times—*and* for helping me work through my intro block. You're the best!

Michael McIntyre, bless your heart for rescuing me whenever the computer gremlins got me. I would have been in serious trouble without you.

David Masters, my other computer guru (but not a Mac man . . . *yet*), thank you for your help with the photographs, our Web site, and our stationery—the "Rocker Chick" rules!

Emily De Huff, thank you for your editing expertise.

Bobby at Mates, thank you for getting that elusive signature!

And a special thank you to Andy Earle and Norman Seeff for sharing those fabulous images with us.

To my friends who helped me deal with the emotional highs and lows of this project (thank goodness they were mostly highs—weren't they?), I am ever grateful for your support: Deanna Clarkson, Valerie Sorrentino, Shahri Masters, Pam Simpkins, Diane Brown, Verlyn Cutler, Patty Eikam, Bob and Chris Blanchard, Stephen Barr, and My Sistahs of Perpetual Indulgence—Joi, Alex, Chris, Suzanne, Laurel, Peggy, Shawn, Libby . . . you know who you are!

To my family for their encouragement and excitement: Lynner—you are the best sister anyone could ask for—the Texas Barkers, Greg Barker, Dan Barker, Jennifer Barker, and my Dad, Gordon Barker, Sr. And . . . from Heaven above, thank you Mom and Scottie, I *know* you were up there helping me! (Oh yes! And Bob, also.)

Most important of all, to David—husband *extraordinaire*, my rock, my sounding board—thank you for your unending support and help (especially with those stinking intros!). You are the perfect partner and I thank God every day I get to share my life with you.

To Jasper—my sweet angel—I thank you for your patience with me when I couldn't play; I love you with all my heart. Isis, thank you for your company while lying sprawled out all over my desk making work just *a bit* more challenging.

Sabu, my other furry baby, thank you for sitting on my lap so I couldn't get up to photocopy or fax anything! *Meow!* To the Fabulous Four, your guidance and wisdom go way beyond words.

And finally, to Margie, thank you for your patience, guidance, words of encouragement, and trust. It has been an amazing experience to embark on this journey with you, one filled with joy and blessings. . . . We did it!

Margie's VIPs

To Cindy Coverdale, your exquisite presence, passion, faith and joy brought this dream to life. I'm amazed . . . now let's have fun!

To Ambrosia Healy, I hope you enjoy my *last* cookbook—I adore you.

To my family and friends on this playground called life who cheered me on: Michael Joseph Beiser, Kate Towle, Denyse and Paul Hughes, Shivani Grail, Kelly Douglass, Cathy Norris, Naomi Petrushka, Ame Beanland, Brenda Knight, Cassidy Law, Shannon Horn, Linda Azar, Nina Lesowitz, Mary Ellen Lord, Susan and Fred Strachan, Tana Hafner-Burton, Rose Hayden, Chris Blanchard, Terry Little, Michael Shapiro, Wayne Pate, Izi Jerman, Potter Polk, Lilly Graber, and everyone in my heart. . . .

To Dorismarie Welcher, Queen of the Hudson, goddess of jazz.

To Vojko and Lila, who love me, inspire me and let me be free to create and dream—I cherish you.

As always, to my muses—my music, my friends, my saints and angels, The Lake, Notre Dame, the Holy Spirit, and Joe Beiser—listening to you, I get the music.

In memory of Jay Kahn . . . rock on in heaven, friend.

The Incredible, Edible Band: Groups with "Food Names"

Ambrosia

Angry Salad

The Apples in Stereo

Back Burner Blues Band

Bananas at Large

The Banana Splits

Beefcake

Big Sugar

Billy Bacon & the Forbidden Pigs

Black Cherry Soda

Black Eyed Peas

Black Grape

Blind Melon

Blue Nectar Band

Blue Öyster Cult

Bondage Fruit

Bowling for Soup

Brandy

Bread

Bread & Butter

The Breakfast Club

Buckwheat Zydeco

Burnt Sugar

Burnt Taters

Burnt Toast

Cake

CakeLike

Candy Snatchers

Canned Heat

Caviar

Cheese

Cheese & Pickle

The Cheeseballs

Cheeseburger Choir

Cheesecake

Cherry Poppin' Daddies

Cherry Twister

Chicken Shack

Chilli

Chocolate C.O.W.Z.

Chocolate Genius

The Chocolate Watch Band

Citizen Fish

Clambake 2000

Coffee

Colossal Pomegranate

Cookie

Corn Doggie Dog

Country Joe and the Fish

The Crabs

Cracker

The Cranberries

Cream

The Crumbs

Cupcakes

The Dripping Lips

The Electric Prunes

Everclear

Fattburger

Fiona Apple

The Flying Burrito Brothers

Gordy Brown and the Bonus Fries

Happy Apple

Honeyz

Hot Lunch

Hot Tuna

Ice Cube

Ice-T

The Jam

Jambalaya Cajun Band

James "Super Chikan" Johnson

Jello Biafra

Jelly Roll Kings

Kilgore Trout

King Biscuit Boy

Kingfish

King Prawn

Korn

Lambchop

Las Ketchup

Leftover Salmon

Lemonbabies

Lemon D

Lemon Drop Kid

The Lemon Drops

Lemongrass

The Lemonheads

Lemon Jelly

The Lemon Kittens

Limp Bizkit

Lovin' Spoonful

Mango Jam

Mango Punch

Marmalade

Meat Loaf

Microwave Dave & the Nukes

Midnight Oil

Moby Grape

Mumbo Gumbo

The Neanderthal Spongecake

Nectarine No. 9

Olive

The Peaches

Peaches & Herb

Peanut Butter Conspiracy

Phish

Red Hot Chili Peppers

Reel Big Fish

Salt-N-Pepa

The Samples

Savoy Truffle

Seltzer

Scary Chicken

Seafood

Skillet

The Smashing Pumpkins

Soup

Spice Girls

Spoon

Stew

Sticky Fingaz

Strawberry Alarm Clock

String Cheese Incident

Sugababes

Sugar Shack

The Sugar Shoppe

Sweet Cherry

Tangerine Dream

T-Bone Walker

Tea Leaf Green

The Tea Party

Tonic

Vanilla Fudge

Vanilla Ice

Zac Zolar and Electric Banana

Tune into Food: Songs with "Food Names"

"Alan's Psychedelic Breakfast"

"American Pie"

"Angel Food Cake"

"Animal Crackers"

"Another Piece of Meat"

"Apple Peaches Pumpkin Pie"

"Apples, Peaches, Bananas and Pears"

"Astronaut Food"

"Baby Lemonade"

"Bacon Fat"

"Baked-Bean Boogie"

"Banana Puddin'"

"Banana Pudding"

"Bar B Q"

"Beans and Cornbread"

"Beans in My Ears"

"Beef Jerky"

"Big Butter and Egg Man"

"Big Fat Ham"

"Big Mexican Dinner"

"Biscuit Eater"

"Black Licorice"

"Bloody Mary"

"Blueberry Hill"

"Blues for the Barbecue"

"Bread & Butter"

"Bread & Water"

"Breakfast in America"

"Breakfast in Bed"

"Bring Home the Bacon"

"Broccoli"

"Bun & Cheese"

"Burgers & Fries"

"Butter"

"Call Any Vegetable"

"Candy Everybody Wants"

"Candyman"

"Candy Store Rock"

"Catfish Blues"

"Catfish Sam'ich"

"Cheese & Onions"

"Cheeseburger in Paradise"

"Cherry, Cherry"

"Cherry Coke"

"Cherry Pie"

"Chicken Cordon Blues"

"Chicken Gumbo"

"Chicken Soup"

"Chicken Stuff"

"Chili Song"

"Chinese Kitchen"

"Chocolate Cake"

"Chop Suey Louie"

"Cinnamon"

"Cinnamon Girl"

"Coca-Cola Cowboy"

"Cockles & Mussels"

"Coconut"

"Cornbread, Molasses & Sassafras Tea"

"Corn Dogs"

"Cornflake Girl"

"Country Ham & Red Gravy"

"Country Pie"

"Cream"

"Custard Pie"

"Cut the Cake"

"Dead Shrimp Blues"

"Devil's Food"

"Dill Pickle Rag I"

"Dinner for One Please James"

"Dinner with Gershwin"

"Donut Man"

"Drinkin' Wine"

"Easter Dinner"

"Eat a Peach"

"Eat It"

"Eat to the Beat"

"Eggplant"

"Eggplant Pizza"

"The Eggplant That Ate Chicago"

"Fast Food"

"First Bratwurst of Summer"

"Fish & Chips"

"Food Glorious Food"

"Food Phone Gas Lodging"

"Fort Worth Hambone Blues"

"Forty Cups of Coffee"

"Fried Chicken"

"Gimme a Pigfoot"

"Gimme Some Water"

"Go for Soda"

"Guacamole"

"Gravy"

"Greasy Grit Gravy"

"Green Onions"

"Grits Ain't Groceries"

"Homegrown Tomatoes"

"Honey Bun"

"Honey Pie"

"Hot Cakes"

"Hot Chili"

"Hot Chili Mama"

"Hot Dog"

"Hot Dogs & Cabbage"

"Hot Dogs & Hamburgers"

"Hot Nuts"

"Hot Pastrami"

"Hot Peanuts"

"Hot Tamale"

"Hot Tamale Baby"

"How Sweet It Is"

"Hungry"

"Hungry Like the Wolf"

"I Am a Pizza"

"Ice Cream"

"Ice Cream Castles"

"I Heard It Through the Grapevine"

"I Love Rocky Road"

"I'm Putting All My Eggs in One Basket"

"Incense and Peppermints"

"Instant Coffee Blues"

"I Want Candy"

"Jambalaya"

"Jam Up, Jelly Tight"

"Jumbo Malt"

"Junk Food Junkie"

"Kidney Stew Blues"

"Lady Marmalade"

"Lasagna"

"Leftovers"

"Lemon Song"

"Life Is a Minestrone"

"Lollipop"

"Lumpy Gravy"

"Macon Hambone Blues"

"Main Course"

"Margaritaville"

"Mayonnaise"

"Memphis Jellyroll"

"Memphis Soul Stew"

"Mother Popcorn"

"Muffin Man"

"My Baby Likes My Butter on Her Gritz"

"My Bologna"

"No Biscuit Blues"

"No Milk Today"

"No Rice, No Peas, No Coconut Oil"

"No Sugar Tonight"

"Old Kidney Stew Is Fine"

"One Bad Apple"

"One Meat Ball"

"One Meatball"

"Onion Roll"

"Onions"

"On the Good Ship Lollipop"

"On Top of Spaghetti"

"Orange"

"Orange Sherbert"

"Oreo Cookie Blues"

"Pass the Pickle"

"Pasta on the Mountain"

"Peaches"

"Peaches en Regalia"

"Peanut Butter"

"Peanut Butter Conspiracy"

"Peanut Butter Time"

"Peanuts"

"Picnic in the Jungle"

"Piece of the Pie"

"Pigmeat Is What I Crave"

"Pink Champagne"

"Pizza on the Ground"

"Polish Sausage Polka"

"Popcorn"

"Popcorn Pop Pop"

"Popcorn, Pretzels & Beer Waltz"

"Popsicle"

"Popsicles & Icicles"

"Popsicle Toes"

"Porcupine Pie"

"Pork & Beans"

"Pork Chop Blues"

"Pork Chops & Gravy"

"Pork Chop Stomp"

"Potato Chips"

"Poundcake"

"Pour Some Sugar on Me"

"Pretzel Logic"

"Pretzel Man"

"Psychedelic Lollipop"

"Quiche Lorraine"

"Quiche Woman in a Barbecue Town"

"Rainbow Stew"

"Raspberry Beret"

"Raspberry Swirl"

"Red Beans"

"Red Beans & Rice"

"Red Hot Chicken"

"Red Wine"

"Reno Burrito"

"Rib Joint"

"Rice & Peas"

"Rice Pudding"

"Rock & Roll Stew"

"Rock Candy"

"Rock Lobster"

"Rubber Bisquit"

"Rum & Coca-Cola"

"Rutabaga Pie"

"Safe as Milk"

"Salt Peanuts"

"Sangria Wine"

"Sashimi"

"Sassafras Roots"

"Saturday Night Fish Fry"

"Savoy Truffle"

"Scottish Tea"

"Scrambled Eggs"

"Shanghai Noodle Factory"

"Shortenin' Bread"

"Soup for One"

"Soup of the Day"

"St. Alphonzo's Pancake Breakfast"

"Stir It Up"

"Strange Brew"

"Strawberry Fields Forever"

"Struttin' with Some Barbecue"

"Sugar & Spice"

"Sugar Pie Honey Bunch"

"Sugar Shack"

"Sugar, Sugar"

"Sukiyaki"

"Sunshine, Lollipops & Rainbows"

"Swamp Sauce"

"Swedish Meatball"

"Swedish Pastry"

"Sweet as Bear Meat"

"Sweet Burgundy"

"Sweeter Than Chocolate"

"Sweet Gingerbread Man"

"Sweet Kentucky Ham"

"Sweet Pea"

"Sweet Potato Pie"

"Sweets for My Sweet"

"Taco Grande"

"Tacos"

"Taco Wagon"

"Tapioca Tundra"

"Taste of Chocolate"

"A Taste of Honey"

"Tastes Just Like Chicken"

"T-Bone Blues"

"Tennessee Fish Fry"

"Texas Cookin'"

"Texas Stew"

"Thanks for the Pepperoni"

"They Call Me the Popcorn Man"

"3 Martini Lunch"

"Tijuana Sauerkraut"

"Too Much Barbeque"

"Top Hat Bar & Grille"

"Tortillas & Beans"

"TV Dinners"

"Two Triple Cheese, Side Order of Fries"

"Vanilla Fudge"

"Veal Chop & Pork Chop"

"Vegetables"

"Waldo's Discount Donuts"

"Watermelon Dream"

"Watermelon Hanging on the Vine"

"Wedding Cake"

"When Did We Have Sauerkraut?"

"When the Cooke Jar Is Empty"

"Wild Honey"

"Wild Honey Pie"

"Wild Mountain Honey"

"Wild Mountain Thyme"

"Wild Rice"

"Wine, Women & Song"

"Worst Pies in London"

All Access

Rockin' Resources

We are proudly donating proceeds from *Food That Rocks* to Freedom from Hunger, a U.S.-based organization that helps women and their families in developing countries break free from poverty by promoting sustainable lifestyles through financial assistance in education, health management, and microenterprise business development.

For additional information, please contact:

Freedom From Hunger
1644 DaVinci Court
Davis, CA 95616
Phone: (800) 708-2555
E-mail: info@freefromhunger.org
www.freedomfromhunger.org

Restaurants That Rock

Croce's Restaurant & Jazz Bar
Ingrid Croce
802 Fifth Avenue
San Diego, CA 92101
Phone: (619) 232-2891
www.croces.com

La Ferme

Gilles LaGourgue and Chef Yves Gigot
2291 Main Street
P.O. Box 97
Genoa, NV 89411-0097
Phone: (775) 783-1001
www.La-Ferme.net

Madre's

897 Granite Drive
Pasadena, CA 91101
Phone: (626) 744-0900
www.madresrestaurante.com

McCoy's

Chef Eugene McCoy
The Tontine, Staddlebridge
Near Northallerton, North Yorkshire, DL6 3JB
Great Britain
Phone: (01609) 882671
www.mccoysatthetontine.co.uk

Mount Blue Restaurant

707 Main Street
Norwell, MA 02061
Phone: (781) 659-0050
www.mountblue.com

Pizza Antica

Gordon Drysdale
334 Santana Row
San Jose, CA 95128
Phone: (408) 557-8373
www.pizzaantica.com

The Tea Room at the Clarence

6-8 Wellington Quay
Dublin 2
Ireland
Phone: (353) 1 407 0813
www.theclarence.ie

A Delicious Experience

The Inn of Imagination

A Bed & Breakfast Experience
470 Randolph Street
Napa, CA 94559
Phone (707) 224-7772
E-mail: info@innofimagination.com
www.innofimagination.com

La Ve Lee Jazz Club

12514 Ventura Boulevard
Studio City, CA 91604
Phone: (818) 980-8158
www.laveleejazzclub.com

Seasons Catering

Stacy Aldrich

Phone: (818) 516-1296

E-mail: stacymae10@aol.com

Catering, event coordinating, and wine consulting

Books That Rock

Ben Fong-Torres

Not Fade Away: A Backstage Pass to 20 Years of Rock & Roll

The Rice Room: Growing Up Chinese-American: From Number Two Son to Rock 'N' Roll

The Hits Just Keep on Coming: The History of Top 40 Radio

You can find Ben's books at bookstores everywhere and online at his Web site: *www.benfongtorres.com*

Ben & Jerry

Ben & Jerry's Homemade Ice Cream & Dessert Book by Ben Cohen & Jerry Greenfield with Nancy J. Stevens

Ben & Jerry's Homemade, Inc.
Phone: (802) 846-1500
To find the book, more tasty links, and lots of fun stuff, visit their Web site at:
www.benjerry.com
www.onesweetwhirled.org

Ingrid Croce

Thyme in a Bottle: Memories and Recipes from Croce's Restaurant

www.croces.com

www.jimcroce.com

For more information and to purchase a copy of *Thyme in a Bottle*, please call (619) 232-4338 or inquire by e-mail to merchandise@croces.com.

Kathi Kamen Goldmark

And My Shoes Keep Walking Back to You

The Great Rock & Roll Joke Book by Kathi Kamen Goldmark with Dave Marsh

Midlife Confidential by the Rock Bottom Remainders

"Don't Quit Your Day Job" Records Web site: *www.dqydj.com*
To order a copy of *And My Shoes Keep Walking Back to You*, visit *www.chroniclebooks.com* (where you can download some of her songs). To order other titles, visit your favorite bookstore or online bookstores.

Patti LaBelle

LaBelle Cuisine: Recipes to Sing About by Patti LaBelle with Laura B. Randolph

Patti LaBelle's Lite Cuisine: Over 100 Dishes with To-Die-For Taste Made with To-Live-For Recipes by Patti LaBelle, Laura Randolph Lancaster

Patti's Pearls: Lessons in Living Genuinely, Joyfully, Generously by Patti LaBelle, Laura Randolph Lancaster

Don't Block the Blessings: Revelations of a Lifetime by Patti LaBelle, Laura Randolph Lancaster

www.pattilabelle.com
Available at most bookstores and online bookstores.

Ted Nugent

Kill It & Grill It by Ted and Shemane Nugent

God, Guns & Rock 'N' Roll by Ted Nugent with Ward Parker

You can purchase a copy of Ted's books at *www.tednugent.com* or *www.amazon.com*.

Tasty Swag

Bob Weir

Weir's Sauces

Hot sauces and cooking oils

www.weirsauces.com
Contact: kim@weirsauces.com
All net profits from the sales of Weir's Sauces benefit the Furthur Foundation, which supports the environment, children's education, and homeless causes.

Joe Perry

Rock Your World Boneyard Brew Hot Sauce

Available at select gourmet shops and via Web site:
www.joeperrysrockyourworld.com

Players' Hot Links

Alex Ligertwood
www.alexligertwood.com

Ben Fong-Torres
www.benfongtorres.com
www.asianconnections.com

Billy Corgan
www.zwan.com

Bob Kastelic
www.nnba.org (Northern Nevada Bluegrass Association)

Brian May
www.queenonline.com

David Coverdale
www.davidcoverdale.com
www.whitesnake.com

Donna Lewis
www.donnalewis.com

Doug Aldrich
www.dougaldrich.com

Doug Bossi
www.dougbossi.com

Doug "Cosmo" Clifford
www.creedence-revisited.com

Eric Martin
www.ericmartin.com

Eric Singer
www.eric-singer.com
www.ericsinger.de

Frankie Banali
www.frankiebanali.com

Gordon Drysdale
www.pizzaantica.com

Gregg Bissonette
www.GreggBissonette.com
www.favorednations.com

Jamie Moses
www.jamiemoses.com

Jan & Dean
www.jananddean.com
www.surfcityallstars.com

Jennifer Lopez
www.jenniferlopez.com
www.madresrestaurante.com

Jim Croce
www.jimcroce.com
www.croces.com

Joe Lynn Turner
www.joelynnturner.com

Joe Perry
www.joeperrysrockyourworld.com

www.aerosmith.com

Joe Satriani
www.satriani.com

Joey Altman
www.foodnetwork.com

John Lodge
www.johnlodge.com
www.moodyblues.co.uk

John Wesley Harding
www.wesweb.net

Jon Butcher
www.jonbutcher.com

Kathi Kamen Goldmark
www.dqydj.com

Larry Hoppen
www.larryhoppen.com
www.orleansonline.com

Lauren Broersma-Cutler
www.bluenectarband.com

Leo Sayer
www.leosayer.com

Leslie West
www.lesliewest.com
www.edromanguitars.com (Ed Roman World Class Guitars)

Lisa Walker, Media Relations Specialist
www.tothemax1.com

Marco Mendoza
www.marcomendoza.com

Max Volume
www.kozzradio.com

Michael Tobias
www.mtdbass.com

Nate Mendel
www.foofighters.com

Patti LaBelle
www.pattilabelle.com

Paul Young
www.paul-young.com
www.lospacaminos.com

Peter Rivera
www.rareearth.com

Reb Beach
www.rebbeach.com

Sarah McLachlan
www.sarahmclachlan.com

Shania Twain
www.shaniatwain.com

Spike Edney
www.sasband.com
www.queenonline.com

Stan Harrison
www.StanHarrison.com

Steve Lukather
www.toto99.com

Steve Vai
www.favorednations.com

Ted Nugent
www.tednugent.com

Timothy Drury
www.timothydrury.com

Tommy Aldridge
www.tommyaldridge.com

Tony Franklin
www.tonyfranklin.com

Tony Hadley
www.tonyhadley.com

Tyler Haugum
www.bluenectarband.com

U2
www.u2.com

Will Hale
www.willhale.com

To all of you currently without hot links, we thank you so very much for sharing your time, your thoughts, your music, and most of all your recipes!

Adrian Vandenberg

Andy Hamilton

Brett Tuggle

Charlie McGimsey

Chuck Bürgi

Colby Leonard for Mike Love

Derek Hilland

Jacqueline Pierce

Patti Russo

Rickey Medlocke

Steve Hamilton

Vinnie Pantaleoni

Hospitality Suite

Permissions

We are grateful for permission to excerpt from the following works and for the delicious recipes, luscious comments, and hearty enthusiasm everyone shared:

Recipe Credits

"The 'Sizzling Penne & Double Truffle' Blues Gratin" and text reprinted with permission of Adrian Vandenberg.

"Uncle Omar's Famous Cliff Sauce with Flank Steak" and text reprinted with permission of Alex Ligertwood.

"Pappardelle Genovese," "Tiramisu," and text reprinted with permission of Andy Hamilton.

"Bul Kogi" and text reprinted with permission of Ben Fong-Torres.

"Russian Salad" and text reprinted with permission of Billy Corgan.

"Basic Bread" and text reprinted with permission of Bob Kastelic.

"Filet Mignon with Tequila and Poblaño Chile Sauce" and text reprinted with permission of Brett Tuggle.

"My Mum's Blackberry Purée" reprinted with permission of Brian May.

"Hot Rod Hot Dogs" and text reprinted with permission of Charlie Girsch.

"Garlic Rubbed Rock & Roll Rib Steak" and text reprinted with permission of Charlie McGimsey.

"Baked Stuffed Avocados" and text reprinted with permission of Chuck Bürgi.

"Ginger-Lime-Cilantro Marinade with Halibut" and text reprinted with permission of Colby Leonard.

"Soulful Shrimp Soup" and text reprinted with permission of David Coverdale.

"Derek's Burritos" and text reprinted with permission of Derek Hilland.

"Welsh Cakes" and text reprinted with permission of Donna Lewis.

"Spicy Coleslaw," "Potatoes Gratin with Bacon, Arugula, and Caramelized Onions," "Pork Tenderloin Salad," and text reprinted with permission of Doug Aldrich.

"Pasta Alle Bossi," "Pizza Bread," and text reprinted with permission of Doug Bossi.

"Grilled Sea Bass" and text reprinted with permission of Doug Clifford.

"Asian Chicken Salad" and text reprinted with permission of Eric Martin.

"Spicy Chicken Pasta" and text reprinted with permission of Eric Singer.

"Sticky Toffee Pudding Cake" and text reprinted with permission of Eugene McCoy.

"Linguini and Clams Castellamare" and text reprinted with permission of Frankie Banali.

"Zen Master DJ Mix" and text reprinted with permission of Glennn
  "Max Volume" Bailey.

"Brussels Sprouts Salad," "Pennsylvania Funnel Cakes," and text reprinted
  with permission of Gordon Drysdale.

"Curried Pumpkin Soup" and text reprinted with permission of
  Gregg Bissonette.

"Seared Hawaiian Ahi with Japanese Salsa" from *Thyme in a Bottle: Memories
  and Recipes from Croce's Restaurant* reprinted with permission of
  Ingrid Croce.

"Desdemona's Island Pie" and text reprinted with permission of
  Kim Thomas at the Inn of Imagination.

"Meringue Torte" and text reprinted with permission of
  Jacqueline Pierce.

"Musician's Popcorn" and text reprinted with permission of Jamie Moses.

"Joe's Italian Meat Sauce for Pasta" and text reprinted with permission of
  Joe Lynn Turner.

"Steak & Eggs" and text reprinted with permission of Joe Perry.

"Shrimp Scampi Pasta" and text reprinted with permission of Joe Satriani.

"Sweet Potato–Plantain Soup with Coconut and Rum Cream," "Yucatan Pork
  Chile", "Chile Maple Glazed Pork Tenderloin with Braised Red Cabbage
  and Sweet Potato Purée," "Oozing Chocolate Soufflé Cake," and text
  reprinted with permission of Joey Altman.

"Lamb Rogan Josh" and text reprinted with permission of John Lodge.

"Not My Curry Recipe" and text reprinted with permission of
    John Wesley Harding.

"John X's Big, Fat, Greek Leg of Lamb with Occasional Potato" and text
    reprinted with permission of John X Volaitis.

"Gaggie's White Potato Pie" and text reprinted with permission of
    Jon Butcher.

"Sweet Lorraine's Chocolate Swirl Cheesecake" and text reprinted with
    permission of Kathi Kamen Goldmark.

"Green Tips Asparagus Vinaigrette with Poached Egg Mousseline,"
    "La Crème Brûlée de la Ferme" and text reprinted with permission of
    La Ferme and Yves Gigot.

"Shrimp with Pasta in Sour Cream and Tomato Sauce" and text reprinted
    with permission of Larry Hoppen.

"Chocolate Tofu Pudding" and text reprinted with permission of
    Lauren Broersma-Cutler.

"Donatella's Special Tuna Pasta" and text reprinted with permission of
    Leo Sayer.

"Tour Bus Tuna" and text reprinted with permission of Leslie West.

"Nana Barnello's Marinara Sauce" and text reprinted with permission of
    Lisa Walker.

"Empañadas Fritas, Crema De Frijoles Negros and Arroz Con Pollo" and text
    reprinted with permission of Madre's/Chef Rolando Gonzales.

"Mama's Ceviche" and text reprinted with permission of Marco Mendoza.

"Sun-Dried Tomato Pesto" and text reprinted with permission of Michael Tobias.

"Pea Soup" and text reprinted with permission of Nate Mendel.

"Potato Salad" and text reprinted with permission of Patti LaBelle.

"Chicken Saltimbocca" and text reprinted with permission of Patti Russo.

"Chicken Escalope with Cajun Mustard Sauce" and text reprinted with permission of Paul Young.

"Seared Tuna with Pasta" and text reprinted with the permission of Peter Rivera.

"Spicy Chicken Wingers," "Veal with Lime Sauce" and text reprinted with permission of Reb Beach.

"Southern Sloppy Buffalo Burgers" and text reprinted with permission of Rickey Medlocke.

"Currant Cake" and text reprinted with permission of Sarah McLachlan.

"Shania's Potato Roast" and text reprinted with permission of Shania Twain.

"Uncle Spikey's 'Honeylamb' Chili" and text reprinted with permission of Spike Edney.

"Oven BBQ Brisket" and text reprinted with permission of Stan Harrison.

"Oatmeal Honey-Butter Biscuits," "Steve's Sticky Banana," and text reprinted with permission of Steve Vai.

"Stevie's Meatballs" and text reprinted with permission of Steve Hamilton.

"Mr. and Mrs. Steve Lukather's Cherry Cheesecake 2002" reprinted with permission of Steve Lukather.

"Caramelised Halibut with Parmesan and Herb Gnocchi, Mousserons, and Sweetcorn Velouté" and text reprinted with permission of chef Anthony Ely/The Tea Room.

"Spanokopita" and text reprinted with permission of Timothy Drury.

"Potato Leek Soup" and text reprinted with permission of Tommy Aldridge.

"Franklin's Outstanding Oatmeal" or "FOO" and text reprinted with permission of Tony Franklin.

"Whole Fresh Salmon à la Chinese Style" and text reprinted with permission of Tony Hadley.

"Ty Peanut Sauce with Rice and Veggies" and text reprinted with permission of Tyler Haugum.

"Vinster Codzini" and text reprinted with permission of Vinnie Pantaleoni.

"Yummy Banana Bread," "Peanut Butter on Toast Sandwiches with Corn Chips," and text reprinted with permission of Will Hale.

"Bubble Bean Piranha à la Colorado Moose" from *Kill It & Grill It* by Ted & Shemane Nugent. © 2002 by Projectile Marketing, LLC. Reprinted with permission of Regnery Publishing, Inc.

Food Men Love by Margie Lapanja. " 2001 by Margaret Beiser Lapanja. Reprinted with permission of Conari Press, an imprint of Red Wheel/Weiser, LLC.

Romancing the Stove by Margie Lapanja. " 1998, 2002 by Margaret Beiser Lapanja.Reprinted with permission of Conari Press, an imprint of Red Wheel/Weiser, LLC.

"*Supermarket Fantasy*" © 2001 by Kathi Kamen Goldmark, from *And My Shoes Keep Walking Back to You* by Kathi Kamen Goldmark (Chronicle Books, 2002). Reprinted with permission of Kathi Kamen Goldmark.

Photo Credits

Permission to reprint photographic image of Adrian and Mickey Vandenberg given by Adrian Vandenberg; photo credit unknown.

Permission to reprint photographic image of Alex Ligertwood given by Alex Ligertwood; photo credit to Neal Adams.

Permission to reprint photographic image of Andy Hamilton given by Andy Hamilton; photo credit to Belinda Pisker.

Permission to reprint photographic image of the Back Burner Blues Band given by Joey Altman; photo credit to Joey Altman.

Permission to reprint photographic image of Billy Corgan given by Billy Corgan; photo credit unknown.

Permission to reprint photographic image of Brian May given by Sara Bricusse; photo credit to Jill Furmanovsky.

Permission to reprint photographic image of Charlie McGimsey given by Charlie McGimsey; photo credit to Charlie McGimsey.

Permission to reprint photographic image of Chuck Bürgi given by
Chuck Bürgi; photo credit to Troy Bystrom.

Permission to reprint photographic image of Cindy Coverdale and
Margie Lapanja given by Susan Zweigle of Zweigle/Ratiner Studios.

Permission to reprint two photographic images of David Coverdale given by
Norman Seeff; photo credit to Norman Seeff for both photos.

Permission to reprint photographic image of Derek Hilland given by
Derek Hilland; photo credit unknown.

Permission given to reprint photographic image of Donna Lewis given by
Andy Earl; photo credit to Andy Earl.

Permission to reprint photographic image of Doug Aldrich given by
Doug Aldrich; photo credit to Stacy Aldrich.

Permission given to reprint photographic image of Doug and Stacy Aldrich
given by Stacy Aldrich; photo credit to Elizabeth Chaumette/
Getty Images.

Permission to reprint photographic image of Doug and Caroline Bossi given
by Caroline Bossi; photo credit to Caroline Bossi.

Permission to reprint photographic image of Doug "Cosmo" Clifford given
by Doug Clifford; photo credit to Laurie Clifford.

Permission to reprint photographic image of Eric Martin given by Eric
Martin; photo credit to Yutaka Nishimura.

Permission to reprint photographic image of Frankie Banali given by
Frankie Banali; photo credit to Glenn Laferman for Trauma Music Ltd.

Permission to reprint photographic image of Glennn "Max Volume" Bailey given by Glenn "Max Volume" Bailey; photo credit to Kelly Kage.

Permission to reprint photographic image of Gregg Bissonette given by Gregg Bissonette; photo credit to Alex Solca.

Permission to reprint photographic image of Ingrid Croce given by Ingrid Croce; photo credit to Mary Kristen.

Permission to reprint photographic image of Jacqueline Pierce given by Jacqueline Pierce; photo credit to Lisa Kohler.

Permission to reprint three photographic images of Jamie Moses given by Jamie Moses; photo credits unknown for all three photos.

Permission to reprint photographic image of Joe Lynn Turner given by Joe Lynn Turner; photo credit to Lisa Walker/To The Max.

Permission to reprint photographic image of Joe Perry given by Joe Perry; photo credit to Ross Halfin.

Permission to reprint photographic image of Joe Satriani given by Paolo Massetti; photo credit to Paolo Massetti.

Permission to reprint photographic image of John Lodge given by John Lodge; photo credit to Brian Aris.

Permission to reprint photographic image of John Wesley Harding given by Cathy Hendrix for John Wesley Harding; photo credit to Abbey Tyson.

Permission to reprint photographic image of John X given by Jessica Janiewicz; photo credit to Jessica Janiewicz.

Permission to reprint photographic image of Jon Butcher given by
     Jon Butcher; photo credit unknown.

Permission to reprint photographic image of Larry Hoppen given by
     Larry Hoppen; photo credit to Darren McGee.

Permission to reprint photographic image of Leo Sayer given by Leo Sayer;
     photo credit to Donatella Piccinetti.

Permission to reprint photographic image of Leslie West given by Leslie
     West; photo credit unknown.

Permission to reprint photographic image of Marco Mendoza given by
     Marco Mendoza; photo credit to Leah Mendoza.

Permission to reprint photographic image of Nate Mendel given by
     Nate Mendel; photo credit to Anton Corbijn.

Permission to reprint photographic image of Patti LaBelle given by
     Patti LaBelle; photo credit to Albert Sanchez.

Permission to reprint photographic image of Patti Russo given by Patti
     Russo; photo credit to Ms. Horsman (London).

Permission to reprint photographic image of Paul Young given by Paul
     Young; photo credit unknown.

Permission to reprint photographic image of Peter Rivera given by
     Peter Rivera; photo credit unknown.

Permission to reprint two photographic images of Reb Beach given by
     Reb Beach; photo credits unknown for both photos.

Permission to reprint photographic image of Rickey Medlocke given by
     Frank Stancliff; photo credit to Frank Stancliff.

Permission to reprint photographic image of Shania Twain given by
Eileen Lange; photo credit to Barry Hollywood.

Permission to reprint two photographic images of Spike Edney given by
Spike Edney; photo credit unknown for both photos.

Permission to reprint photographic image of Stan and Chloe Harrison given
by Stan Harrison; photo credit to Margot Steinberg-Harrison.

Permission to reprint photographic image of Steve Lukather given by
Anita Heilig; photo credit to Robert Knight.

Permission to reprint photographic image of Steve and Pia Vai given by
Glenda Kravets; photo credit to Glenda Kravetz.

Permission to reprint photographic image of Timothy Drury given by
Timothy Drury; photo credit to Jerry Tarshis.

Permission to reprint photographic image of Tommy Aldridge given by
Karen Aldridge; photo credit unknown.

Permission to reprint photographic image of Tony Franklin given by
Tony Franklin; photo credit to Robert Knight.

Permission to reprint photographic image of Vinnie Pantaleoni given by
Vinnie Pataleoni; photo credit to Joanne Stassi.

Permission to reprint photographic image of Will Hale given by Will Hale;
photo credit to Greg Wanbaugh.

Permission to reprint photographic image of Yves Gigot, David Coverdale,
and Gilles LaGourgue given by Yves Gigot, David Coverdale, and
Gilles LaGourgue; photo credit to David Masters.

Set List

Index

Artists listed alphabetically by first name.

About the Authors

Margie Lapanja, author of *Food Men Love*, *The Goddess' Guide to Love*, and *Romancing the Stove*, loves rock 'n' roll music and is dedicated to stirring up more fun, love, and pleasure in life through her writing. She has lived other incarnations as a kitchen goddess, magazine editor, food writer and restaurant critic, professional baker and bakery owner, aphrodisiac expert, and love-advice columnist, exploring all things sensuous and spiritual. She lives life lusciously at Lake Tahoe in Nevada.

First-time author Cindy Coverdale is delighted to be involved in a project that blends together two of her favorite passions—music and charity. Married to singer David Coverdale of Whitesnake, Deep Purple, and Coverdale/Page, Cindy has been exposed to the intimate, inner world of rock 'n' roll and is grateful to be able to utilize this experience as a way to inspire and help others in a joy-filled forum. She makes her home with her husband, their son, and two designer kitties in the Sierra Nevada Mountains overlooking Lake Tahoe.

Please visit our website at *www.foodthatrocks.com*.

To Our Readers

Conari Press, an imprint of Red Wheel/Weiser, publishes books on topics ranging from spirituality, personal growth, and relationships to women's issues, parenting, and social issues. Our mission is to publish quality books that will make a difference in people's lives—how we feel about ourselves and how we relate to one another. We value integrity, compassion, and receptivity, both in the books we publish and in the way we do business.

Our readers are our most important resource, and we value your input, suggestions, and ideas about what you would like to see published. Please feel free to contact us, to request our latest book catalog, or to be added to our mailing list.

Conari Press
An imprint of Red Wheel/Weiser, LLC
P.O. Box 612
York Beach, ME 03910-0612
www.conari.com